PETER LEIGH GANNICOTT

9 May 1960 – 12 May 2005.

A biography by Betty Gannicott
...fulfilling her promise

Betty Gannicott
(Peter's Mum)

www.trafford.com

North America & international
toll-free: 1 888 232 4444 (USA & Canada)
phone: 250 383 6864 ♦ fax: 250 383 6804
email: info@trafford.com

The United Kingdom & Europe
phone: +44 (0)1865 722 113 ♦ local rate: 0845 230 9601
facsimile: +44 (0)1865 722 868 ♦ email: info.uk@trafford.com

10 9 8 7 6 5 4

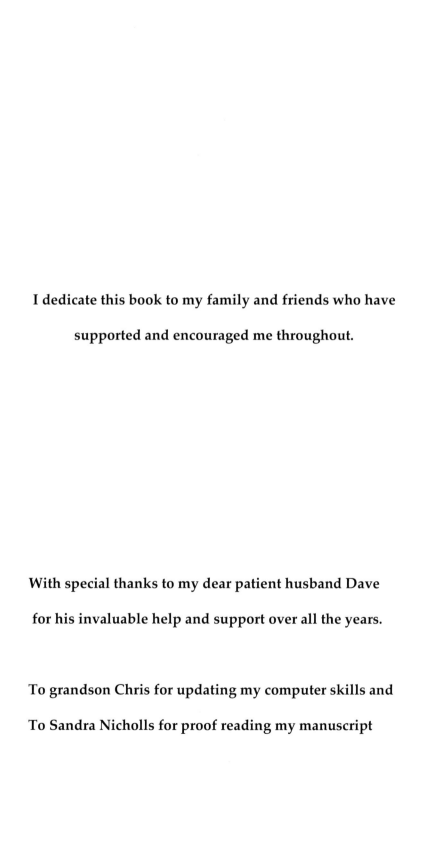

I dedicate this book to my family and friends who have

supported and encouraged me throughout.

With special thanks to my dear patient husband Dave

for his invaluable help and support over all the years.

To grandson Chris for updating my computer skills and

To Sandra Nicholls for proof reading my manuscript

PREFACE

"I will not be having any children who will be able to remember me. I would like to write my autobiography, so I have something to pass on when I die."

Peter spelt out these words to his father one evening when he was visiting him. At first they filled us with melancholy but sadness and pity are negative feelings and not qualities Peter wanted associated with his life. He wasn't courting sympathy but just stating a fact and outlining his ambitions for the future. A mammoth task for Peter though. Even before his accident, he wasn't academically inclined but afterwards, it took a tremendous effort and a great deal of patience on his part just to achieve one or two lines of text.

The idea was mooted but then lay dormant for several years. It took all Peter's energy and determination just to stay alive but the commitment was still there.

Eventually, he asked me to write all I could remember about his early years and whenever possible we would chat together about the latter part of his life with me taking notes and acting as official recorder for him. There was never enough time and the pressures of daily living thwarted his ambitions to become an author.

His story will not now be an autobiography, just a biography with various members of the family helping me out when my memory fails. However, Peter was such a strong character I feel he is looking over my shoulder all the time and as usual, taking overall command of what, after all, is his story.

In fact I did visit a spiritualist a while after Peter's death and without knowing anything about me, during the course of the reading, she mentioned that Peter did know what I was doing and he approved of my writings. This gave me the impetus to get on with his story so Peter, I do hope you like the finished narrative.

CONTENTS

Peter Leigh Gannicott – his story

Part 1

Part 2

Early Years

Peter Leigh Gannicott arrived on 9th May 1960, more like a bat out of hell than from the safety of my womb. He was a week before schedule and I had just about the proverbial four minute warning of his entry into the world.

We already had one son, David, who was almost two years old and we had been trying to prepare him for the arrival of his new sibling. In the event, he nearly had to assist with his delivery!

Peter was nothing like his elder brother who took life very seriously, was a bit shy and had a great need to conform to the rest of his contemporaries. Peter was an exhibitionist. From very early on, he was the clown of the family, who would do just about anything to make people laugh. He hurled himself into everything and never stopped to consider the consequences of his actions. Life to Peter meant the present minute – to be savoured to the full without worrying about tomorrow and what was to come, or yesterday and what had been.

Music and the world of entertainment entranced him even as a toddler. Acker Bilk was his favourite musician for a time, as our neighbours knew to their cost. Peter had a deep brown voice, not particularly melodious but very loud. Every night for some considerable time, around 3 am we were treated to his rendition of 'Stranger on the Shore'. Just the first couple of lines, then a pause before he started again...and again...and again. We were not too popular with our neighbours who were all awakened from their slumbers by our son, who actually sounded more like a drunk returning home after a very heavy night's drinking rather than a sleeping four year old. When we could stand it no longer, we would go into his room and try to wake him up, threatening and pleading alternatively with him to stop the 'singing' so we could all get some sleep. Shame really because I don't think he was ever aware of the trouble he was causing. Another one time idol was George Formby (where he had even heard him was a mystery – he wasn't exactly a pop idol of the sixties) but Peter just had to have a ukulele. He never did learn to play the thing but it was his treasured possession for a long time and he spent hours strumming in the hope he would one day make his debut.

An eye for a bargain

Peter was never a materialist. Whilst David simply just had to have the highly priced elite brand named toys, games, sports gear, clothes etc., according to whatever was the rage at any given time, Peter was content to improvise and use hand-me-downs from his brother or anyone else for that matter. This was just as well because he didn't take care of his possessions and nothing lasted too long. Any item of monetary value was promptly broken, lost, swapped or sold for a pittance.

He did, however, have a keen eye for anything he considered a bargain and occasionally was the envy of others because of an item he had acquired at a jumble sale. Such was the case with the bowler hat. He was assisting on a stall at a cub/scout jumble sale. As a bona fide helper, he was allowed a quick look round before the doors officially opened. As soon as he spied the bowler, he knew he had struck gold. He just had to have it. It was a beautiful bowler, brand new with a white satin lining on which was emblazoned the Royal Coat of Arms and the words 'By Appointment to H.R.H.... followed by the name of the most famous hatters in the business. It was a large bowler – very, very large. Peter wanted to see how it suited him and borrowed a mirror for this purpose. Sadly, this was not possible. As he lifted it on to his head with pride, it slid down over his eyes (and ears and mouth as well, if the truth be told). He was not fazed by this and willingly parted with a whole week's pocket money to clinch the deal. The hat was his. Later in the day, a giant of a man offered him four times what he had paid for the hat but Peter was adamant. The bowler was not for sale. He wouldn't have parted with it for a small fortune.

Peter treasured his bowler. With his vivid imagination, the bowler's possibilities were endless. Each morning it was carefully brushed before the day's activities began and when he finally went to bed, it was laid at the foot, so it was within his sight at all times. We had never known him keep anything for so long without some mishap occurring.

School days

Peter was very eager to start school. When he was four years old we had our third child – a sister for the two boys, Julie Anne. David couldn't wait to go to school the following day to impart his important news, but who could Peter tell? Life was a bit boring for him at home. The new baby took up a lot of my time and David seemed to be doing such exciting things at school. They had a sand pit, played with water and had a percussion band. He went to the school every day to deliver and collect David but wasn't allowed to stay. In fact, they probably wouldn't have wanted him near the place if they had known he was the rascal responsible for making all the little holes in the fresh cement on the newly laid path around the sand pit. I had only left him for a minute while I had a word with David's teacher, but when I returned, I was horrified to see the result of his labours. Apparently all the children had been warned at Assembly not to go near the new path, which was to make a nice edging for the sand pit. Sadly, nobody thought to tell Peter. He had absolutely ruined it with the end of my umbrella. David was so embarrassed.

At last the day dawned when he could start school himself. The first term was fine for Peter but then he decided it wasn't coming up to his expectations. I remember him coming home one day and saying "Mum, how long do I have to go to school for?" My reply must have really disheartened him. The thoughts of having to go every weekday even when the sun was shining coupled with the fact that he was expected to sit still in a classroom and work for at least some of the time, appalled him. He was a free, creative spirit who thrived in the outdoors. Worst of all, the school wasn't even using the same teaching methods as when David started there. They had embarked on a new method for learning to read – 'The initial teaching alphabet' or I.T.A for short. He rebelled against this and wanted to do the same as his brother which he felt would have been a much easier option.

Looking back now, I am also sure that he was dyslexic but this wasn't recognised in 1965. All through his life his spelling was quite bizarre. We taught him to read at home and I will always be grateful to my mother for her daily help with this. Blackmail and bribery were our methods. Peter liked his pocket money **daily**. Three old pennies could buy a Jamboree bag or a tube of sweets from the local shop every day. If he had thirty old pennies a week like his brother, his would all go on the first day and there would be nothing for the rest of the week. He didn't get his daily allowance until he had visited his Grandmother on the way home from school and read to her for ten minutes or so. Then it was straight off to spend his 'fortune'.

Once he could read reasonably well, he tolerated school better but until then it was a real battle of wills each day. The Gannicott household was not a peaceful place to be at 8 am on weekday mornings. How can a six year old cause such pandemonium? His excuses for not being able to go to school matched his vivid imagination. He could suffer anything from a headache, earache, sickness, to pains in his toes; his legs could be stiff or wobbly; the teachers may all be sick so the school had to be closed or the children had been so good they were given a day's holiday. I used to feel a physical wreck by the time I had convinced him he had to get up and go to school. Even then, he could still play his master stroke. Just as we were about to leave the house, with David muttering he did want to be at school early, Julie strapped in her pushchair, Peter would announce he couldn't possibly leave yet as he needed to go to the toilet. This could take for ever. Still, once he actually got beyond the school gates, things

6

were fine; a truce was declared until the following morning. My sympathies go out to all parents who suffer similar problems.

Apart from school Monday to Friday, we also **thought** he went to Sunday school although it transpired that this was not actually the case. I am afraid he was the ring leader of a small gang including my sister's three younger children. When we dropped them at the entrance to the Church premises, they would only pretend to go in but usually managed to avoid detection and could disappear from our view. Once the coast was clear, they would make their way to the nearby river Ching to play, stopping en route to buy sweets with the money given to them for the collection box. This went on for some time until we became suspicious as to how their Sunday best clothes could get so grubby whilst they were in church and decided to check up on our offspring.

Unlike his elder brother, Peter was not really keen on cricket or football. I remember him saying there was only one thing more boring than watching football and that was being expected to play the game himself. In spite of his feelings on this subject, he did accompany his grandfather and David to see Leyton Orient whenever they had home fixtures, for a whole season on Saturday afternoons. The reason for this was not actually to see the game but something far more important. Grand-dad always took a supply of sweets to the match and would also buy the boys a hot dog at half time. Peter became a lapsed supporter after my father agreed to give him the cash in lieu of his ticket, so he didn't have to feign interest any more.

Peter's sporting achievements centred on and around water. He could swim long before he could read and write and gained quite a few medals for his prowess in this sport. The diving board was the reason for him breaking his front tooth. I was sitting in the spectators' gallery, watching and wondering why he kept diving in the water. Eventually he surfaced and yelled out to me "Mum, I've broken my front tooth but I've got the bit". He couldn't understand why the dentist couldn't glue it back in position.

Fishing featured prominently from an early age. I clearly remember his first rod and line. He was seven years old and we all went on holiday to Llanaber, a small seaside resort about three miles from Barmouth, at the mouth of the Mawddach Estuary. It was an idyllic spot and we rented a large caravan perched on high ground, overlooking the sea. It was May time, the scenery was breathtaking and the weather just perfect. The boys thought the caravan was fabulous and we more or less had the whole site to ourselves.

There was only one problem. We had no sooner arrived when Dave developed a raging temperature and very badly inflamed throat. It was obvious, even to the boys (who could hardly wait to explore their new environs) that plans would have to be altered. I really felt their dad should seek advice from a doctor, but the car was parked on a steep incline and I didn't feel confident about moving it. I decided it would be far simpler to walk along the beach to Barmouth itself where there would be a doctor's surgery, taking the three children with me. This would give their father a bit of peace and quiet and them the chance to release some of their pent up energy.

Julie, who was only three years old, said she would walk providing she could wear her red Wellington boots and the boys wanted to take their new fishing rods....just in case. It was a boiling hot day and we must have looked a motley collection as we entered the surgery. Julie was clad in a little bikini and the boots; the boys were in swimming trunks but bare footed, (we had forgotten footwear for when we had to leave the beach) and me, dishevelled and anxious looking, clutching two fishing rods which the boys had long since tired of carrying.

Doctor Jones was very sympathetic and remained quite serious in spite of the state of us all. He thought he really should see Dave before prescribing for him and said he would call at the caravan later in the day. We said our goodbyes and all trekked back along the beach without the boys even having a chance to test their fishing rods. I needed to get back and await the doctor's visit. The diagnosis was a bad attack of tonsillitis and for the treatment to be effective, he would have to stay in bed at least for a few days. Dr. Jones told the boys if they were really good and looked after their dad, he would hopefully be able to take them out after five days. I didn't like leaving Dave for too long and the boys weren't old enough to venture forth on their own so we didn't go far while he was sick. Rather earlier than suggested and due I suspect to the constant queries from the boys as to the state of his health, Dave declared himself much better and ready to go out. We wouldn't go far, just to a suitable place on the Mawddach Estuary so the boys could use their fishing rods.

I think Peter had visions of a record catch. He had armed himself with a large bucket for his fish, some bread for bait and a good measure of optimism and enthusiasm. Unfortunately, he was incapable of standing still himself, let alone whilst holding a rod. After about ten minutes, without so much as a bite, he was getting decidedly bored. His concentration lapsed and he started annoying his brother. One poke led to another and before long our attention was diverted from amusing Julie to the sight of raised rods and angry shouts from David. Their lines were hopelessly entangled. They let go at our admonishments and both rods seemed lost forever as they quickly floated downstream towards the sea. Maybe the cost of replacement was uppermost in their father's mind, or the thought of trying to placate Peter, who was bawling his eyes out; either way, they all got drenched in the rescue operation and that was the end of fishing for the day.

Dad didn't fare any better later the same day. After changing into dry clothes, he was teaching David to skim stones along the water, to see how many times you could make them bounce – 'ducks and drakes' I think it is called. Peter was keen to join in but hadn't a clue what to do. Somehow his stone managed to leave his hand in backward flight and catch his father full force around his eye. Not a promising start to his convalescence – a dousing and a black eye. He would have done better had he taken the doctor's advice and had another day in bed!

David building and Peter demolishing

Peter's first school photo

Sporting his broken front tooth

How did he manage to get a prefect's badge?

As a teenager

Scouting for boys

Peter couldn't wait to become a cub scout. As far as he was concerned, they did such exciting things in this organisation and he was very fortunate because the local leader and his assistant were extraordinarily dedicated people who gave a great deal of their time to the young boys in their care. They encouraged and nurtured his enquiring mind, spirit of adventure, love of nature and the wild outdoors. In addition, the international home of scouting at Gilwell Park was on our doorstep and camping under canvas soon became a most important part of Peter's young life. He progressed from cubs to scouts where he was also very lucky with the adult leaders of his unit. He never lost his interest and enthusiasm for scouting although sometimes the rules had to be slightly adapted to accommodate his own unique personality.

An eventful camp

Peter was a member of the Gilwell Park Scout Camp Work Management Team, from the age of about fourteen. For quite a time he spent most of his weekends and evenings there. He took part in various conservation projects, general maintenance of the site, painting and decorating etc. He wasn't particularly skilful but was very strong and thrived on the manual work in the outdoors. It also meant he had certain privileges and could camp there without too much adult supervision. I am afraid school homework did suffer as a result but this suffered anyway. It was proving an impossible task to get Peter to sit still and do any studying. At least while he was at Gilwell, there wasn't the usual conflict of opinions as to where he could go, who with, how long he could stay etc.

On one particular occasion, Gordon, one of Dave's brother's sons from Virginia, U.S.A. was staying with us for the summer. I was going to be away for a week with my brownie pack. Julie would be coming with me and David Junior and Dave would both be at work. Peter and Gordon made plans to camp at Gilwell during this time, which seemed an excellent idea. Colin, a scouting friend of Peter's decided to join them and they all got together to work out the equipment needed and menus for the week. Food always played a most important part in their camping expeditions.

Colin was a nice lad, quite clever I believe, but slightly eccentric. They showed me their menus. "Wouldn't it be easier to use a **tinned** syrup pudding?" I enquired, thinking of the time it would take to cook one from basic ingredients. "Mrs Gannicott", said Colin in a voice filled with shock and horror at the prospect. "A ready made tinned one, you just have to heat up?" "Well, it would save you time and a steamed pudding would take hours to cook, let alone prepare", I murmured, wishing I hadn't mentioned the matter. "Well, you haven't tasted **my** steamed syrup pudding" he said, "It's out of this world".

I never did get confirmation of the gastronomic ecstasy of Colin's steamed pudding as Peter and Gordon didn't actually manage to sample some, so were unable to give their opinions. Colin prepared it alright and got as far as starting to cook it over their Gaz stove. (Scouts have long been converted from the old wood fires it seems). Now all their training in camping skills and safety precautions deserted them. They became bored. There were other things to do more pressing and of greater interest than sitting watching a steamed pudding cook. Beside, the wind was affecting the efficiency of the Gaz stove. They had a quick conference and decided on a plan. They would move the stove to the doorway of the store tent and protect it further from the wind by making a shield with their precious cases of Coca Cola. Coke to Gordon, the American lad, was a vital necessity of life. He never went anywhere without an ample supply of the stuff and camping at Gilwell Park was no exception.

No sooner the word and the deed was done. Then they made a tragic error. They forgot to anchor the tent flap back securely. Worse still, they didn't even stop to see the result of their labours, or clear up the mess around the store tent. There were cooking utensils, camping gadgets, various paraphernalia and even their precious transistor radio, all strewn around the doorway. They reasoned nobody was likely to interfere with their things. Scouts have respect for other people's property – but not their own it seems. We'll clear up later they promised themselves as they headed off to see what amenities the camp had to offer.

Alas, they hadn't gone far before a gust of wind caught the tent flap and blew it straight on to the burner. The sound of numerous coke cans exploding brought the boys hurrying back to the scene. The fire was quickly brought under control but the damage was considerable. All their coke had gone and the radio was reduced to a small lump of molten plastic. Items that hadn't been destroyed by fire or water had been ruined by a pack of cub scouts, hell bent on carrying out their good deed for the day, who had come charging through, making a better job of flattening everything than a bulldozer could have done. Also, of course, there was the small matter of the store tent, which was a total write off. Peter had borrowed this from his scout troop and they would need it shortly for their own camp. Fortunately, it was insured, but replacement takes time. They decided they would have to come home and go and make their apologies.

Not only did scouting suit Peter's love of the outdoor life but it also gave him a compassion for others, highlighting his natural ability to care for those less able than himself. For many years from quite a young age, he would take part in camps and holidays specially designed for physically or mentally disabled lads. We were a bit concerned at first that maybe he was a bit young to be spending so much of his free time in this way but he loved being involved. He learned many procedures as a carer, albeit a very young one, which ironically he would need carried out for him after his accident. He had the patience to feed someone, wash and clean up after them, rather enjoying the mess and didn't panic if something went wrong. Yes, he became good at first aid and had understanding far beyond his years. Nevertheless, he didn't worry about the problems these youngsters had or let their disabilities upset him. His sense of humour and ability to see the best in everything and everybody stood him in good stead and made him an ideal candidate for this kind of service.

Another aspect of Peter's involvement with scouting was entertainment. Each year they practiced and put on a 'Gang Show' at a local venue. I'm not sure this helped his academic progress at school and once again, his homework definitely suffered. Why did rehearsals always coincide with times when he was supposed to be revising hard for an exam?

As soon as they would have him, Peter joined the Forest Venture Unit (a branch of scouting which also included girls – a bonus as far as Peter was concerned). Sir Stuart Mallinson, a local dignitary, had given them a large hut on his land in the forest to renovate and use as their own. Peter learned quite a few D.I.Y. skills on this project and many other things as well, I am sure! He appreciated the feeling of complete freedom and slept at their hut most weekends. Cold weather did not deter these boys and girls; in fact the majority including Peter, used to head for Snowdonia each Boxing Day morning and camped in the mountains, which were normally covered in snow by the time they arrived. I am not sure how much time was spent in the local inns having a little something to keep out the cold but to be fair, I think they all enjoyed trekking in the clean fresh air in this beautiful part of Great Britain. I know Peter did anyway.

Teenage Years

By his early teens, Peter's unique personality and character were well established. It was always a challenge to know the best way of guiding and disciplining him without crushing his spirit. He just had a different concept to the rest of his peers as to what was the right and wrong way of going about things. He was not very interested in school work although could charm all the young female teachers even to the extent of getting their co-operation in excusing his various escapades. He was a great swimmer and was awarded a gold medal at least once for his prowess in a county event. Alas, we never even got to see this as by the time he reached home he had already sold the award to a friend for a few pence, so he could buy a packet of crisps. He dealt with life as it came along; was not interested in possessions but always made the best of what he had. In this case, the packet of crisps was more of an asset than a gold medal.

He had a fascination for taking things to pieces to see how they functioned – clocks, watches and electrical appliances were his passion and their owners were not usually consulted before he took them apart with the aid of one of his father's screwdrivers. Was he going to become a famous inventor? Alas, no! Once Peter got his hands on something, the result was usually that it never worked again. His brother was so exasperated at his sibling's lack of regard for what was to him, his treasured possessions, he insisted on having a lock put on his wardrobe door to keep Peter and his meddling fingers out.

What would he be able to do with his life after he left school at sixteen? There was no point in him staying on for further education. It would be like trying to cage a wild bird. He liked the natural world, outdoors pursuits, talking to everyone, and sport (apart from cricket and football). The career's master at school thought he would probably eventually make a first class community policeman always providing he could pass the entrance examination to become a police cadet. This appealed to Peter and he worked very hard for a while so he could sit the examination. His Scouting activities and achievements looked very good on his application and he was most pleased to hear he had passed the written test and was to be given an interview and medical. Then came a catastrophe; we just couldn't understand how he had passed everything else with flying colours but had failed the medical. In 1975 the Metropolitan Police did not accept cadets who required spectacles and Peter had failed the eye test which was included in the medical examination. Our optician was puzzled and even managed to get him a retake but he failed the sight test again. I still wonder if this had something to do with him being dyslexic rather than having poor vision. He could try again in another year but meanwhile, what could he do with his life?

He did have lots of disco equipment and actually got paid on occasions for providing the music for events but his outlays always far exceeded anything he earned from this venture. Mostly his bookings were for friends or acquaintances that he couldn't possibly charge for his services, or even ask for reimbursement of his expenses to cover transporting all the heavy gear to a venue. "Mum" he would say, "I have to get well known first and then I will make a lot of money. You will see. I need to speculate before I can accumulate."

I am not sure how or why, but he managed to get offered a position as a clerk with the Inland Revenue in London. Most unsuitable for Peter really but he decided they had good recreational facilities, a canteen and as an added bonus, he would get one day off per week to continue with his educational studies. We were not quite sure how improving his skills with a snooker cue at the local club qualified under the heading of 'academic subjects' but it made the post bearable for him and it was **paid** employment and therefore a proper job. The big drawback was that he had to stay indoors and for the most part, sit at a desk and at the very least **look** as though he was working.

I was not surprised though when a few months later I received a telephone call from him at my office. "Mum" he said. "I've handed in my notice at work. I'll die if I have to be a civil servant for very much longer or I'll end up do something dreadful, and then I won't even get a reference. I want to come to America with you and dad when you go on holiday next month. I've got it all worked out. I will have my final wage cheque and this will pay for my air fare. Then, when we come home I have a new job lined up with the local council working as a Play Leader."

We had booked flights some time earlier to see Dave's family in Virginia. In the first instance, we wanted the boys to come with us but they were adamant. This year, they were spending their holiday entitlement camping with their own friends. They wanted to be independent. We therefore arranged for my parents to look after the boys while Julie and ourselves were away. Peter, as usual, hadn't any reserve funds. Nothing had changed. As soon as he had any cash in his pocket, it had to be spent but as he explained, he didn't need any money to have a good time with his cousins in the USA. The first time we visited the family, all his dollars had been stolen on the day he arrived in America but he still had a wonderful holiday, so what was so different now? There was no point in arguing with him, what could we say?

In actual fact it transpired that he didn't actually have a job to go to on his return from America; it was just an idea forming in that crazy head of his. Yes, he could work at the parks, as an assistant play leader but it was on a **voluntary** basis without any remuneration. The young people who used the Parks were mainly juveniles with problems and Peter liked the challenge. There were no petty rules and regulations; he didn't have to be up early or wear a collar and tie; he was able to use his own initiative and best of all, he could go to work on his skate board and show off his skills and tricks with this when he arrived at the Park. In due course, he was offered paid employment in the Adventure Parks as a bona fide Assistant Play Leader.   He was over the moon. The money was not very good but he loved the work and found the kids who used the parks challenging. It seemed a good stop gap until he could apply again to join the police force.   In the event, he met Eldita who also came to work as an assistant at the parks and all thoughts of becoming a police cadet evaporated into thin air.

Eldita

Peter always liked to introduce us to his girl friends very early on in their relationship and so it was with Eldita. I think he had only been out with her a couple of times when he brought her along to a family gathering at a London restaurant. We liked Eldita straight away with her long blond hair, dimples, dancing eyes and ready smile but wondered how long she would put up with Peter, especially after he managed to upset a bottle of red wine all down the front of her beautiful new white dress. She handled the mishap magnificently though and didn't make any fuss about returning to the table in a now almost transparent frock; the result of Julie's endeavours to try and sponge it down in the ladies toilets. Peter could charm the proverbial hind legs off a donkey and was so romantic. I remember the pair of them returning to our house after a walk around the block, Ellie looking dewy-eyed holding a fresh red rose close to her face. It wasn't until I questioned Peter later that I learned he had picked the rose from a neighbour's front garden to give to Ellie swearing his undying love for her. I don't think our neighbour was too impressed though – he was a gardening enthusiast and the rose was one of his prize blooms!

It wasn't very long before we knew things were serious between the two of them. They both still worked together at the Adventure Playground and in addition, were also spending most of their free time in each other's company. However, we were a bit concerned when Peter told us he wanted to take her to Virginia, U.S.A. to live there for a while. He was only just nineteen years old and with his madcap way of life we couldn't imagine he was responsible enough to look after himself away from home, let alone a girl who was even younger. How could they get work without the obligatory 'green card' and what would the family in Lynchburg think about it all? We couldn't even be sure he wouldn't find an American lass he liked better and then desert his English rose. We had a meeting with her parents and tried to express our concerns to them. However they explained that their daughter was very strong willed and once she had made up her mind to do something, there was nothing they could say to deter her. If Peter ditched her in the States, then so be it; she would have to come home alone.

In the end the two young love birds went with the blessing of both families and we just expressed the hope they would look after each other. At least Dave's family would give them bed and board while they sorted themselves out. As it happened they didn't stay with the family in Lynchburg, Virginia, for too long before they had both managed to get jobs and find an apartment of their own fairly close to the city college where there were plenty of young people about and the type of entertainment they enjoyed. Peter took an American driving test and they bought an old car so they could travel around a bit. I know they were very happy most of the time they spent in the U.S.A. although occasionally they both suffered with spells of homesickness.

Peter worked for a 'butcher block' furniture making company owned by a Mexican couple (probably they didn't have green cards either!). The money wasn't great but nobody asked any questions about their status or entitlement to be working in the U.S.A. We did visit whilst they were in Virginia and took Peter and Ellie to Florida for a week's holiday before we returned to the U.K. They seemed so happy together and had grown up a lot since they left England. In hindsight, how glad we were that they had this year and a half together before they married – not quite the norm in 1979 but at least they were able to fulfil a few dreams before tragedy struck.

Whether our stay had anything to do with their decision to leave America, I am not quite sure but a short while after our visit, we had a telephone call from Peter to say they were thinking of returning home. I thought he said they would probably spend some time in Spain first doing some casual work 'grave digging' to improve their cash flow. When I relayed this information to Ellie's Spanish father however, he fell about laughing; I couldn't understand what he found so funny but then I was unaware of the usual custom in his homeland at that time, for disposing of their dearly departed loved ones. Apparently their ashes are placed in an urn and put in a niche at a cemetery or churchyard. Therefore there would be no call for grave diggers. What Peter and Ellie actually had in mind was to earn some money **grape picking.** They knew some people who had a vineyard and thought they could stay with them and help with the grape harvest. In the event they decided against this idea and came straight home instead. They wanted to get married and didn't have time for grape picking or grave digging come to that! As was customary with Peter, once he made his mind up about something, there was no time to lose.

They flew back to the U.K. with plans for their future formulated. Temporarily, Peter came to live with us at home and Ellie returned to her Mum and Dad's abode. Wedding bells were not far off though but first they both had to find work again. The travel bug had bitten them and they planned to save hard once they were married, so they could visit Peru next, paddling a canoe down the river Amazon through uncharted swamps, where unfamiliar creatures abounded and there was the whiff of danger in the air. Their dream was not to participate in an organised sightseeing tour although they did want to visit the land of the Incas etc., but in their own style, travelling rough and going where their fancy took them. Sadly, this ambition was not realised for Peter although I believe Ellie did manage a slightly more civilised and watered down package trip to South America two or three years after Peter's accident.

Meanwhile, his first priority was to find paid employment. He now had some experience in woodwork and got a job with a company making cabinets. His heart wasn't really in this though and when he heard that a local record shop was looking for an assistant manager, he applied for the position and was accepted. He had a lot of knowledge about the music scene and he knew he would enjoy the work. It paid as well as the cabinet maker and significantly better than the Adventure Playground. If he was going to have to take a mortgage on a home of their own and save for their proposed trip, he realised a reasonable wage would be of prime importance.

Although they had already lived together for eighteen months, they wanted their wedding to follow old fashioned traditions and he formally asked Jaime (Ellie's father) for her hand in marriage before they finalised their plans. They were marrying on Valentine's Day, 14th February 1981 which dawned bright, sunny and reasonably warm for the time of year. The ceremony took place at St. John's Church on the Green in Chingford witnessed by all their friends and families. It was a very impromptu affair and being practical for once, Peter didn't want to waste his money on a suit he would never wear afterwards, so he borrowed one of his dad's for the occasion. Ellie wore a very pretty three quarter length chiffon dress and she carried a bouquet of carnations. She looked so young and very beautiful when she arrived at the church on the arm of her father. Afterwards we all adjourned to her parents' house for the reception. One of Peter's favourite American cousins, Danny, had been staying with us for a while and we were able to persuade him to delay his return to the U.S.A. so he could attend the ceremony. I still have a vivid memory of Danny lying under the wedding breakfast table later in the day, consuming the carnations which had made up Ellie's bouquet, due I fear to his having partaken of rather too much alcohol. I think we decided it was best to leave him there until the next morning. As Ellie said, she had finished with her bouquet and he was welcome to it if that is what satisfied him. It would leave more food for everybody else and she didn't really care. She was married to Peter now and they were both very happy and contented with just each other's company.

Eldita – taken soon after their arrival in U.S.A.

Outside the family's house in Lynchburg, Virginia.

Married life

Peter and Ellie had finally been offered a mortgage on a suitable flat which they could afford in Walthamstow, and they moved in, both blissfully happy with the way their lives were turning out. Ellie was a good homemaker and although they didn't have expensive possessions, they were both more than satisfied with their first proper home together in England.

One day when they were having dinner with us, the subject of Peter's twenty-first birthday came up. He still had all his disco equipment and wanted to celebrate his official coming of age with a party to remember. As he explained, the problem would be finding a suitable location. He realised their flat wouldn't be big enough and in any case, it wasn't soundproof and they didn't want to upset their new neighbours (after all they had only moved into the road a couple of months earlier). They couldn't really afford to hire a venue and so did we have any suggestions? Was it a possibility he could hold it at our house where there would be enough room for his all important disco equipment as well as people? I think he already had it planned and as usual, we fell straight into his trap. It was just a formality asking us for the use of our house for his celebrations and so it was arranged.

The party was a huge success and we have lovely memories of Peter standing behind his record deck, whilst gyrating to all his favourite reggae music, his headphones in place and a glass of his home brewed beer at the ready. Whenever I hear 'Jamming' by Bob Marley, I am immediately transported back to that party. I will never forget the look of sheer ecstasy on his face and am so glad we agreed to it all. He came round the next afternoon, looking very worried to enquire about any damage, cigarette burns and the clearing up. He was always an expert at turning on the charm and his display of concern was just an act to make sure we wouldn't be too cross about anything but how could we be? It had turned out to be such a lovely party.

Brewing his own beer quickly became a favourite hobby of Peter's even if the end result didn't always turn out exactly as planned. His brother reminded me of the time he telephoned him to invite him round that very same evening for a few beers. David already had plans for that night but said he would go the next day. "No" said Peter – "it has to be tonight or the beer will be off". It transpired the barrels had exploded and he had 100 pints of beer in the bath to be consumed by the next morning. Good job that Ellie had a similar laid back personality.

They both loved the forest and Sundays were often spent bicycling through the woods before arriving at our home for a family roast or a barbeque. David and Sue, who married just seven months later, would also join us and Julie too when she was around. Uncanny really, but David and Sue married exactly one year before Peter's dreadful accident on the 26th September 1982.

However, 1981 was a good year for the family and there was to be yet one more wedding before Peter's accident. My sister's only daughter Debbie was married to Steve on the 6th August 1982 – yet another opportunity for Peter to volunteer to concoct his Home Brew although I am not sure the wedding guests were too impressed with the lethal potion.

One incident occurred which upset Dave and I far more than it did the newly weds. They were burgled and most of their few belongings of any value, stolen. We were so upset when we went to inspect the now somewhat empty flat and I couldn't help shedding a tear or two, especially when I saw the vacant spot where all his precious music system had previously occupied pride of place. "Don't get upset Mum" said Peter. "It's only possessions and they can always be replaced". In the event, they did get some of the stolen property back as the culprit was seen by a neighbour and identified as a local man. When the police went to the thief's house to question him, he still had quite a few of their goods, all on plain view and he was cheeky enough not only to have been playing one of their records but on their stereo machine as well!

Peter had managed to acquire a very old car – rather a wreck I'm afraid but it served its purpose I suppose and allowed them to get around when their bikes or his skate board were not appropriate for a proposed journey. (I know he still used either of the former modes of transport to get back and forth to work). He still hadn't passed an English driving test though and it worried his dad and I to think he only had an American licence. He assured us this was legal and he was entitled to drive for a few months on a U.S. licence but he wasn't an American citizen and we weren't so sure therefore, that these regulations applied to him. We paid for a few lessons and an English test which fortunately he passed at his first attempt. At least this gave us some peace of mind and meant we could sleep easier in our beds. We thought it would be cheaper in the long run rather than run the risk of having to bail him out of jail.

They enjoyed entertaining friends and families in their flat, individually contributing to the catering which nearly always had an International flavour. Eldita and Peter were both good cooks and they liked experimenting with different recipes. Maybe this was how he first developed his love of very hot and spicy foods which were to play such an important part in his later life when they were a necessary part of his diet. Whatever food was served, there was always a plentiful supply of home brew to go with it plus much laughter and lots of chatter.

We were invited to have dinner with them both just a couple of days before we left on a routine holiday visit to Dave's family in Virginia that fateful September in 1982. After dinner, Peter said he had something to show us. He was very excited but also rather apprehensive and we wondered what on earth he wanted us to see. When we did finally get to view this thing which was the cause of his great excitement and concern, my heart went cold as we realised he had bought a motorcycle. We were horrified but what could we do? He was married now and we had no say in how he spent his money or what he did with his life. Until he left home, we had always fought against him having a motor cycle as we knew it would become a lethal mode of transport under his control.

Peter had no fear of danger and we felt he would only thrill to the speed and power a motorcycle could give him without due consideration as to what the result of his actions might be. He said this motorbike wasn't a very powerful machine, and it was incapable of doing high speeds even if he wanted it to do so – he joked that he would wait till he was proficient before thinking about saving for a Harley Davidson and until that time, we shouldn't worry. However, he would be very careful and safety would be uppermost in his mind when he was riding the present machine. All we could do now was to reiterate our fears and hope he would have the good sense to be extremely careful and mindful of our warnings. I don't think Ellie was too happy about the situation either but I know there wasn't much she could do about things once Peter had made his mind up. We finally left that evening with heavy hearts and great fears for his safety in spite of his reassurances that he was a grown man and knew what he was doing. Our parting pleas to him were to be careful and make sure he was still there in one piece on our return from the United States. Sadly, this was the last time we saw Peter before his appalling accident.

Peter and Eldita on their wedding day

PART TWO

The Accident

26th September 1982 – The day Peter sustained his dreadful and most horrific road traffic accident.

Peter was going to see a friend of his who lived locally on this fateful Sunday morning, accompanied by his younger cousin, Stephen. Both of them had only recently acquired their motorcycles but the machines were road worthy, they had their licences and were wearing proper crash helmets. As is typical of young men, however, they were full of confidence and probably travelling rather too fast for the prevailing road conditions. The injuries Peter suffered when he lost control and went into the side of a car could hardly have been more devastating and the consequences of the accident changed his life completely and for ever.

From this day forward until his death nearly twenty three years later, he would never be able to make so much as a sound let alone speak. He would be totally paralysed, unable to move any part of his body or limbs. Even to do something as normal as breathing would be beyond his capabilities, without some form of mechanical assistance and he would be dependent on other people to perform even the most basic of tasks. It became a mammoth operation for him just to make someone understand if he needed his nose wiped or his chin scratched. Although it was not apparent at the time, he had suffered a brain stem injury which resulted in what is commonly known as 'locked in muscle syndrome'. His brain stem had been crushed so messages were unable to pass through it in answer to his commands.

At the time, by coincidence, a 'flying' doctor was in the immediate vicinity of the crash and came to Peter's aid, carrying out emergency resuscitation at the kerbside until an ambulance arrived on the scene. He was then taken to the Accident and Emergency Department of Whipps Cross Hospital, just a few minutes drive away. By the time Eldita and other family members arrived at the hospital, it was becoming apparent that Peter's injuries were very very serious. Apart from superficial cuts and bruises, there wasn't really a lot to see but the number of staff tending him and the look on their faces told a different story. My sister, Joan, thought David needed to telephone us in America to alert us as to what had happened. I know he didn't find this an easy task, and it was made even more onerous by the fact that his dad was out with his own brother when he rang so he had to give the dreadful news directly to me.

Before we left for our holiday with the family in Virginia, the orthopaedic surgeon I worked for had enquired if there was anything he could do for me whilst we were away. This was because I used to water his house plants and keep an eye on his home whilst he was away. However, his words came flooding back to me whilst I was speaking to David. I asked him to get in touch with John to see if there was anything he could do to make sure Peter received the very best treatment possible. Meanwhile, it was agreed we should sit tight until there was more news. John liaised with the doctors at Whipps Cross, saw Peter for himself and gave David a progress report. Peter was to be moved to The National Hospital for Nervous Diseases in Queen Square, London, with immediate effect, for treatment by one of their specialist teams. We couldn't ask for more.

At least Peter was alive and we now made urgent plans for our return to England. The earliest possible flights were booked and we were kept right up to date with the situation during our journey home. We knew Peter had been moved to Queen Square and although his hold on life was extremely tenuous, everything possible was being done for him. We were rushed through the formalities at Heathrow and sped by taxi to the hospital where our son was fighting for his life.

David looked rather relieved to see us when we arrived and gave us an up to the minute report before we entered the room where Peter was being nursed. Ellie was by his side, holding back her tears and trying her best to be brave. She looked so young and vulnerable to be facing such a dreadful state of affairs. We would have to put our emotions on hold and try to be strong for her. She needed our support as much as Peter who was lying so still and quiet, surrounded by a battery of complicated machinery. He had already had one emergency operation to relieve some of the pressure in his brain and his head was swathed in bandages. I had never seen so many tubes connected to anyone's body. A nurse moved softly round his bed adjusting the various machines, constantly checking the readings and making notes on the charts ready for the doctor's appraisal. Before this nurse took a break, another was ready to take her place after a detailed hand-over had been carried out.

Before we left to have a few hours sleep, a doctor came to talk to us and he explained what they were trying to do for Peter. The idea was to keep him unconscious for some time which would give the bruising of the brain stem a chance to subside. If all went well, he would gradually be brought back to a conscious state so that eventually he would regain his former good health.

Meanwhile, the surgeon needed to perform a tracheotomy so that ventilation and suctioning of his airways could be carried out more easily. We were assured this was only a temporary measure which could be reversed quite easily when Peter was capable of breathing for himself.

Queen Square

For nearly two years following his horrendous accident, Peter was a patient at The National Hospital for Neurology and Neurosurgery, Queen Square in London – but even whilst he was in intensive care, he never lost his indomitable spirit. He couldn't move, eat, swallow, speak or even breathe without mechanical aid but his brain was as active and sharp as ever. He was kept sedated for a number of weeks to see if the brain stem would heal itself. During this time, as he told me later, he dreamed that he was on a long train journey travelling through India, only gradually becoming aware of the music playing continuously from his cassette player by the side of his bed. Very early on we had been advised to play his favourite music to him as we were told this would probably be the first thing he would hear when he woke up.

The doctors explained to us that they were hopeful Peter's brain stem had just been very badly bruised and given time, it would recover. All the staff looking after him here were marvellous. He had one to one nursing in his own intensive care room for many months before he was finally transferred to a ward but even then, there was no real improvement in his condition. In hindsight the doctors must have known when he was allowed to return to a conscious state, that the brain stem was irreparably damaged and the prognosis was not good. However, Peter and the rest of us laymen were ignorant about the signs and symptoms and remained optimistic he would eventually get better. In any case, we were probably not ready at this stage to accept the fact that he would be so severely disabled for the rest of his life. We were even naïve enough to think that the frequent spasms in his limbs were signs of voluntary movement returning.

Various memories come flooding back to me. He hated being tube fed and longed for a taste of things he used to like. I can remember surreptitious drops of alcohol being added to his tube feed, tasty morsels of favourite food being put in gauze for him to try and suck. Physiotherapists, Speech and Occupational Therapists had sessions with Peter daily. They had tremendous patience and showed such optimism whilst they were with him. He was given a wheelchair and although he couldn't even support his own head, once he was propped up with pillows, he was at least able to visit the gym and other therapy departments thus escaping the confines of the ward for a while. In the gym he was transferred to a mat for exercises and therapy to his limbs. His muscles were rapidly becoming quite wasted due to lack of use. He tried so hard with the speech therapists to improve his chewing and swallowing techniques but he couldn't move his tongue and swallowing was more by luck than judgement. The professionals would have preferred him to have had nil by mouth but Peter was absolutely determined he would eat and drink again. He was adamant and although he couldn't open his mouth more than about half a centimetre at first, he wanted to try. For a long time his dad used to visit him twice each day - before he went to work and in his lunch break and patiently feed him a small bowl of ready-brek. I would then take over later in the day after I had finished work and try to give him some mashed vegetables. Eldita would help when she could but she was also working and anyway, Peter didn't really want to waste precious time when his wife was with him, trying to eat like a baby. Her kisses and cuddles were much more important to him.

He was still under intensive care when his special communication method was devised. He had very expressive eyes still and he used to raise them for 'yes' and lower for 'no'. He could also look very cross if something was wrong and I can still remember the look he gave me whenever I forgot and stroked his arm or cheek. There was no way he wanted pity or his mum treating him like a child. He was his own master and would do things his way. It was extremely frustrating for all his visitors but most of all Peter himself when he could only communicate by a yes/no question and answer method.

One day Stephen, his cousin popped in to see Peter. He worked in London in the fish market, not far from Queen Square but usually he went home first for a shower and change of clothing before visiting. This was to avoid the strong smell of fish permeating throughout the warm environs of the whole hospital. On this particular day, however, he couldn't wait for such niceties. He had very important things to say to his cousin.   "Peter" he announced on his arrival. "Brian and I have been discussing your lack of speech". (Brian was Peter's employer at Master Blaster, the record shop where he worked prior to his accident). "We have got an idea so you will be able to tell us exactly what you want to say" …...and so the alphabet system of communication was borne – an innovation of Brian and Stephen - two young men without any knowledge or experience in the field of communication and speech aids for the disabled; just a strong desire to alleviate some of the frustration felt by their close friend and colleague.

Over the years many different sophisticated means of communication were tried but nothing ever took the place of this simple method of conversing with Peter. The secret of its success was the fact it was personal on a one to one basis. If Peter was 'talking' to you, you had to look at **him**, not stare at a screen or machine to know

50

what he wanted to say. Of course because of his bizarre method of spelling, it sometimes got very complicated and difficult to understand what he actually meant. He was very patient though and providing you tried, he would not give up but go on and on until you understood him. We had an alphabet board placed near his bed for staff and visitors and a goodly supply of pencils and paper to facilitate writing down the letters. Doctors and senior staff never really mastered the system, partly because they were too busy but also due in no small measure to the fact that they didn't like to appear stupid if they made a mistake or couldn't understand. However, junior staff and even the cleaners had a go. (See the alphabet system)

We could soon tell Peter had not lost his sense of humour or his determination to see the funny side of most situations. Various members of staff were likened to different characters. People he had seen on television, movie stars, teachers from his schooldays or the like. Once he had mastered this new means of communication, he could make us all laugh again and this pleased Peter. Also, he was able to be more explicit in his requests even if we didn't always understand what he meant. I had no idea that 'Old Peculiar' was the name of a beer for instance or that 'Frankie Goes to Hollywood' was a pop group.

Of course he got very frustrated at times but we had a pact and he kept his annoyance and grumbles for Dave and me. We were older and better equipped to handle his frustration and loss of patience, which never lasted for long anyway and we didn't want him upsetting Eldita. She was so young and vulnerable and needed supporting herself. I think we knew and I am sure that Peter did, there would come a time when Eldita would have to break free and make a new life for herself but this was in the future and not to be considered now. For the present, it was vital that she gave Peter all the love and support she could. Considering her young age and vulnerability, she coped extremely well with the situation and was most important to Peter's welfare. I'll say one thing though; he taught me some words I didn't even know existed let alone their meaning! So much for the alphabet system but at least it allowed him to release some of his pent up emotions.

If only Peter could breathe on his own without the assistance of the ventilator. Surely that wasn't a lot to ask? Every day he insisted on the ventilator being turned off for a period while he tried to breathe on his own. He was so determined. Sometimes he managed for two or three hours but his breaths were very shallow. You could see the concentration on his face as he willed his lungs to fill with air, but gradually his lips and fingernails turned more and more blue from lack of oxygen and eventually, in spite of his protestations that he could manage, he had to be reconnected to the ventilator. Tomorrow might be better, or maybe not so good......we could only hope for the best. We all became quite expert at interpreting the various signals put out by the complicated machinery surrounding Peter, particularly the respirometer that measured the depth and quality of his breaths. Much as he liked to take chances, even Peter realised he had to get enough oxygen to his brain or it would not function properly. This was the last thing he wanted and so he had to accept the ventilator – at least for the time being.

In these early days Peter had quite a lot of muscle spasm. We couldn't understand why this involuntary movement couldn't be harnessed and serve some useful purpose in the efforts to get him to move again. It was explained to us in layman's terms. To move any part of the body, a message has to be sent from the brain to the appropriate limb, telling it what to do. All messages have to go through the brain stem before reaching their destination and Peter's brain stem was completely mangled so nothing could pass through it. To this day, I am not completely sure whether the medics knew then that his brain stem was damaged beyond repair or if they too hoped for at least some improvement.

Hardly a week went by without some new crisis. He had a thrombosis in his leg and we were told if a clot broke away, it could go straight to his lung or heart. There seemed to be something wrong with one of his kidneys because he was having difficulty passing urine. Chest infections and pneumonia were common place as were eye infections. Even Peter's eyelids didn't work properly and he couldn't close his eyes completely or blink automatically. Therefore, his eyes were very dry and required constant lubrication. It only needed a speck of dust to get into one of them and that eye would become very inflamed; the inflammation then quickly gravitated to the other eye. Eyelids act like car windscreen washers and wipers and without their constant movement, eyeballs really suffer. Peter had already sustained retina damage to one of his following the accident, so he agreed to have the lid partially closed to try and prevent it getting worse. In addition, he also had both eyes taped shut overnight whilst he slept.

There was one particular nurse who Peter didn't like. This was quite unusual for him as he normally saw the best in everybody. I think she felt she knew best and just wanted to do her job without any patient involvement. The other nurses routinely explained what they needed to do before touching Peter and always asked his permission before going ahead. Not so with Tenko (Peter's name for her). His temperature had to be taken either by placing a thermometer in his armpit or his groin instead of under his tongue. This was to avoid the risk of his mouth going into spasm and his teeth clenching on the instrument. In 1982 glass thermometers filled with mercury were still used in hospital. Be that as it may, Tenko came to do

Peter's observations one morning and before Peter could make any protestations, the thermometer had been shoved in his mouth. I do wonder if his mouth went into spasm because he was so cross with her rather than accidentally, but either way, the result was not good. The glass broke and blobs of mercury were everywhere, including Peter's mouth. He must have swallowed some and emergency X-rays had to be taken; yet another crisis! Mercury is a poisonous substance if it gets into the body and can cause a lot of damage. However, thankfully Peter didn't seem to suffer any ill-effects and Tenko was much more careful and considerate to him following this near mishap.

Nearly all of the patients on this ward were very seriously ill; the majority had brain injuries or tumours. As their nearest and dearest, we relatives formed a special bond with each other. We enquired as to how each patient was progressing on a daily basis and their progress became most important to us. We gave sympathy and support to their kith and kin, intuitively knowing if someone felt down in the dumps or there was a crisis with their particular loved one. The hospital became our world; we spent all our spare time there and our conversation and thoughts rarely strayed outside the confines of the ward and its occupants.

Next to Peter was a young Lebanese lad. He had been due to start University but after suffering severe headaches, he was admitted to the private hospital nearby for what was to be fairly routine minor surgery, before starting his studies. However, something went terribly wrong soon after the operation and he developed a brain haemorrhage. Poor Sammy never did get to University nor even walk or talk again. He was in a waking coma for the whole of the time we knew him but his family visited every day, gently encouraging him and never giving up hope of a miracle for their precious son.

There was a family room just outside the main ward where we could go and try to relax, have a coffee and a bite to eat or at least a few serene moments to ourselves, when the pressure of our bedside vigils became too much to bear. One day a couple came in with a young lad of about ten years of age, so boisterous and seemingly full of life unable to sit still for five minutes. His parents didn't try to calm him down or make him behave in a manner appropriate for the relatives' room. I am afraid the rest of us all felt rather aggrieved at his conduct and were not sorry when he was taken off to be admitted to the ward. We so erroneously assumed there couldn't be anything seriously wrong with a boy who was wrecking havoc in what was supposed to be a quiet and peaceful room. Once he was out of earshot, however, his parents told us that their son, who they idolised, had suddenly developed very odd and worrying symptoms. Subsequent investigations had shown a massive malignant tumour on his brain. Surgery was his only hope. Sadly he didn't regain consciousness after his operation and nothing more could be done for him. His parents were so brave and wanted his organs donated. I'll never forget how they waited in the family room for two whole days until potential recipients of their boy's organs could be traced and he could be allowed to die in peace and with dignity.

The days drifted into weeks and then months. Peter was moved out of the surgical ward into one that was more sensitive to coping with people who had breathing problems. We seemed to have reached an impasse and couldn't see any way forward unless Peter could be moved to a hospital specialising in helping people who were paralysed. The consultants at Queen Square didn't object to us contacting a Spinal Unit but they weren't exactly encouraging. However, we were not to be deterred and wrote to Dr. Frankel, the chief consultant at Stoke Mandeville at that time, pleading Peter's case. He explained they didn't normally take people who were ventilator dependent especially when they had so many other problems in addition to paralysis. However, eventually, he agreed to meet Peter and from then on, difficulties were ironed out and transfer to Stoke Mandeville was to be arranged.

A chart explaining the alphabet system:

To chat to me follow these easy steps:

Ask which column (by saying 1, 2, 3 or 4)
When you get to the correct column, I will open my eyes
You now know the column!

Say each letter in the column in turn. Watch my eyes.
When my eyes open wide, you will have a letter.
Write it down before you forget.
Repeat the above steps until eventually you get a word
Two blinks means double letter. Tightly closed eyes means something wrong.

COLUMNS

1	2	3	4
A	H	O	U
B	I	P	V
C	J	Q	W
D	K	R	X
E	L	S	Y
F	M	T	Z
G	N		

Don't forget to look at me – you know the alphabet and only have to remember the start of each column – i.e. A, H, O & U.
Use a pen and paper – it is easy to forget letters otherwise.
Just remember it takes a lot of time to start with and often gets very frustrating trying to chat. Remember I have lots of patience and hope you have too! Good luck.

Note: Eventually, Peter only used his left eyebrow (which he was able to do with relative ease) to communicate, rather than his eyes and he found this less tiring.

Stoke Mandeville

Peter was eventually transferred to Stoke Mandeville on the 1st September 1983 almost a year after his accident, under the care of Dr. Frankel. He was to spend the next two years of his life at this hospital. It was very difficult at first because he couldn't be on the spinal unit overnight whilst using a ventilator. The plan devised for Peter involved him spending his nights in the main hospital on an intensive care ward. Once the morning staff reported for duty, he could transfer to the spinal unit where he could hopefully manage without a ventilator for the majority of the day. He really disliked having to be in intensive care at night. The spinal unit was full of young men who were fun to be with, in spite of the fact that they had all sustained serious accidents. Although the majority were probably going to be paralysed for the rest of their lives, they were part of a special community at Stoke Mandeville all working towards their return to life outside a hospital environment. Peter could only be on the fringes of this because he had to go back to the intensive care unit each evening. Nowadays, the situation has improved and the spinal unit can cope with people on ventilators but this was the early nineteen eighties and a lot has happened concerning patients' care since then.

The unit had recently been entirely rebuilt. Jimmy Savile had been instrumental in raising the vast sum of money required for the rebuild and he had persuaded some large companies to donate things for the refurbishment, fixtures and fittings. He was very much in evidence, strutting around with a huge cigar in his mouth, big chunky rings on his fingers and lots of gold chains around his neck and arms. This image belied the real man though who away from the limelight led quite a simple life. He was very good to Peter, who he called 'the boss' and always came in to see him when he was on the unit. Jim loved the sun and often made use of the sheltered fairly private spot just outside Peter's bedroom window. Here he could gain a brief respite from being watched all the time, due to his celebrity status. Alternatively, if we visited during the evening and the great man was on the ward, he always came to see us, asking what I had cooked for Peter. I got into the habit of taking enough for Jim who especially enjoyed a casserole or anything else if it was home made. Otherwise, I have a feeling he mainly ate ready meals from a motorway service station. Several times he gave Eldita a lift home in his Rolls Royce but he always emphasised if there was anything Peter wanted, we just had to let him know.

Dr. Frankel decided to bring in a neurosurgeon to see Peter. This man (Mr. Peter Teddy, FRCS), was doing pioneering work with American diaphragmatic lung pacemakers which could, if successful, do away with the need for a ventilator. It was a very costly procedure not really available on the N.H.S., but we were told someone was willing to donate the necessary funds. Due to this benefactor 'fixing it' Peter was able to be considered for the implants. The operation was successfully carried out at The Radcliffe Infirmary, Oxford on the 14th December 1983 and eventually this meant, Peter was able to stay on the spinal unit at Stoke Mandeville full time both day and night.

Many years later, after Christopher Reeve had his accident whilst out riding, Peter wrote a very long and detailed letter to him, extolling the worth of his own 'lung pacemakers' and suggesting the actor should investigate their suitability for himself. He never did receive a reply but we noted in the media, 'Superman' did have similar implants inserted into his chest towards the end of 2003, sadly only a year before he died.

Whilst Peter was an inpatient at Stoke, the bombers struck at the Conservative Party Conference at Brighton. Margaret Tebbit was admitted to the Unit and her husband Norman was being cared for at RAF Halton nearby. As soon as he himself was well enough, Norman used to visit his wife and we often met up in the visitors' kitchen, queuing up to use the microwave to heat food for our loved ones. In spite of his own and Margaret's appalling injuries, he always made time to ask about Peter and whether he was making any progress. He never showed any bitterness as to why they themselves had been so afflicted. After all, he had just been fulfilling his duties as a prominent member of the Conservative government. I greatly admired his courage and fortitude during the difficult times which followed the I.R.A. bombing of the Grand Hotel, Brighton where so many important delegates were staying whilst attending the party conference.

Eldita and Peter were starting to drift apart. She didn't visit as often and was talking about life outside. Peter was philosophical about this; they were both young and whereas he didn't have much choice as to what he could do with his life, he never forgot that she could choose. We were terribly worried that he would lose the will to live without her but this was not the case. I think when the break did come it was somewhat of a relief to him. He knew he had to plan his future without her but as he explained to us, this was inevitable really. He just wanted to get on with things. The same day he told us they were going to divorce, Princess Diana visited the unit. Jimmy Savile had brought her along to see what the new wing looked like. Her visit was early morning, completely unannounced and totally without ceremony. As soon as the word got around, senior staff came hurrying in from all directions but they were too late, she had made her visit, chatted with the patients and like a whirlwind, was gone. Peter was very impressed. She came rushing into his room and the staff had no time to warn her or to use a fresh air spray to clear the pungent smell of curry pervading the atmosphere due to him indulging in one of his favourite Indian dishes the previous evening. She just asked him if he was slumming it with his bottle of H.P. sauce, sat on his bed and stroked his hand. Despite the curry, her visit was like a breath of fresh air in the unit.

We had great hopes of amazing progress at Stoke Mandeville but this was not to be for Peter. He realised and accepted the fact that he was not going to make any significant improvements, much quicker than we did. He was now just interested in making the most of the life he had left to him. As far as he was concerned, it was no use wasting time on something he knew would not happen. He was not going to walk or talk unless there were some pretty miraculous medical breakthroughs. Nevertheless, the lung pacemakers were functioning well; they were a great improvement on the cumbersome ventilator over which he had no control. At least the pacemakers were compatible with his own shallow breathing efforts whereas the ventilator prohibited any input from Peter himself. Eating and drinking was also getting a bit easier, providing he concentrated and avoided certain things such as rice, which seemed to get stuck in his throat and always brought on a fit of coughing. As he explained to me, it didn't matter; he could substitute Naan bread or a jacket potato to accompany his beloved hot Indian curry.

The idea of a pillow alarm, which even he could use with his very limited head movement, was initiated by one of his friends who worked in the burglar alarm business. Not being able to speak, it was vital for Peter to be able to summon help if he needed it during the night. Until his pillow alarm was perfected, he was reliant on other bed fellows alerting staff to his needs or the chance of a nurse or somebody passing close enough to his bed to hear the soft tut-tut sound which was all he could make, to signal he required attention. His pillow alarm, which was positioned just under his head, was actually an adapted pressure pad normally fitted inside a home under the front door mat. When the main alarm system in a house was switched on, if anyone stepped over the threshold they couldn't really avoid treading on the concealed pad and activating the buzzer. Peter's model used the same system of pneumatic air pressure but the rubberized pad was smaller and padded so as not to chafe his skin. A lead led from this to a box containing the buzzer with an on/off switch which was hung over the side of his bed. In spite of massive technological advancements over the ensuing years, this simple device was used by Peter every night right up until the time of his death. I think he valued it as one of his most important pieces of equipment.

Computer technology was only in its infancy in the nineteen eighties and not very much had been developed to improve the lives of severely disabled people. Possum Controls were doing sterling work in this field but their equipment for alternative switching devices relied on the person being able to speak, breathe or have some movement and Peter could not fill any of their criteria. At that time, their efforts mainly centred on 'suck/blow' systems using a type of straw instead of a mouse for a switch. Suck in and this acted as one switch and blow for the second part. Peter could suck in but the rest was impossible. He could not blow or even let go of the straw. There were other organisations and charities working on inventions but naturally, financial constraints meant they were not able to spend too much time customizing anything for just one person's use. However, I do remember one particular charity called REMAP who did just that. REMAP was a collection of mainly retired people from many walks of life who gave of their time and expertise in their own field without remuneration. Instead of trying to make an individual fit a piece of equipment, their remit was to make a piece of equipment fit an individual. There was a team of several people from this organisation who worked extremely hard to try and come up with an easy access method for Peter to control his equipment. Unfortunately, in spite of all their efforts, they were not really able to come up with any serviceable ideas for Peter.

He really needed an electric wheelchair that he could propel himself but nothing he could obtain via the NHS was suitable for him then. Eventually after seeing quite a lot of electric models in the private sector, a suitable wheelchair was found, with a chin operated joystick. He was so pleased to take delivery of this because it allowed him to join the other young men in the communal areas without anyone's assistance. He had a version of his pillow alarm fitted in the headrest of the chair so he could now also roam around the whole unit unaccompanied but able to summon aid if needed.

Around the same time, he was given a mini-writer which he could operate with a mouth stick to type simple requests, providing the machine was put in exactly the right position on a table for him to use or eventually on a mounting affixed to the side of his chair. Accessing equipment was always the biggest problem. Peter had such limited useful movement, mainly restricted to his one eyebrow. He did have some control of his head but this could be affected by tiredness or poor oxygen levels when he found it impossible to hold his head up, let alone move it. Spasms could also mean his position changed and suddenly equipment was out of his range.

I remember he needed some dental work done and it was decided this would have to be under general anaesthetic so his mouth could be forced open sufficiently for the treatment to be carried out. Peter spent ages typing his own consent for the operation on his mini-writer but then I was asked to sign a 'proper' standardised form on his behalf. Peter was adamant, if they couldn't accept his consent, he would not have the work done. Of course I agreed with him and this caused quite a stir. The true meaning of independence has come a long way since the nineteen eighties but I am sure this obstinacy stood us both in good stead for when we had to fight for his future 'independent living' in the community.

Eventually we reached a compromise over the consent form and the dental work was carried out. When we saw him after the operation, he told me about his 'out of body' experience. He said he felt like he went down a long corridor and was then floating outside his body. He said it was rather a nice feeling and he was quite happy but eventually people called him back. We rather scoffed this idea and said this was just a normal experience after an operation. However, the anaesthetist asked to see us and said there had been a problem with the ventilator tube, which had kinked on his way back from theatre and Peter's airway had been blocked. Apparently, Peter knew what was happening but because of his lack of speech, he couldn't alert anyone to the situation. The doctor was most apologetic but reassured us he hadn't left our son's side until the emergency was over. Peter's philosophical reaction to the affair was to say he wasn't having any more general anaesthetics unless someone was in theatre who could understand his alphabet system. "I could have died" he said. If we had had any doubts, here was confirmation Peter valued his life and in no way was he ready to give up without a fight.

He also fully intended to carry on as normally as possible in spite of his appalling disabilities. 'Normal' for Peter included turning on the charm whenever there was a pretty young lady around and there were quite a few of these amongst Stoke Mandeville staff. He understood that he wasn't the man Eldita had married but young ladies, who met him after his accident, accepted him for the person he had become. He still had magnetic charm, the most expressive eyes and a somewhat lopsided smile. On several occasions when we visited, we found a young female therapist spending her off-duty time with Peter holding his hand and patiently listening to his stories, which of course had to be carefully spelt out. He wasn't looking for romance but just enjoyed a mild flirtation. It was reassuring to him to know that he hadn't lost the ability to turn on the charm and attract the opposite sex.

I know Peter's disabilities made a lasting impression on many of the young men on the spinal unit. None of them would have been there if their injuries had not been serious but somehow Peter gave them the courage to face up to their own problems. As one of them commented to me, "how can I complain, at least I can speak and breathe for myself". Nevertheless, it can't have been easy for any of them....a professional dancer with a well known group, a famous jockey, a fireman, an Iranian businessman and a lad hoping to make a career in the regular army as a paratrooper...to name but a few. Hopes and dreams for their futures were now in ruins and they would need to plan for quite different lives when they eventually left St. George's Ward on the Spinal Unit.

After he had been at Stoke Mandeville for over a year, Dr. Frankel and his staff started to discuss Peter's future with him. What did he want to do when the time came for him to leave their unit and move on? The wheels had to be put in motion for his eventual departure. Beds at this place were in great demand and could only be occupied by people who could benefit from the special facilities they afforded and who could continue to make improvements.

A conference was arranged to discuss the issues and possibilities for Peter. A date was set when Dr. Frankel was available to chair the meeting and the various therapists, senior nursing staff and other case workers involved could all attend. Dave and I were most concerned and worried about what options would be available for our son but Peter himself took it all in his stride. In actual fact, when we were all seated and ready to commence, Peter announced he needed to speak to me first about something really important. I wondered with trepidation, what he wanted to say and could hardly believe my ears when he explained what he wanted me to do. Apparently he had heard on the radio that tickets for the first Live Aid concert were going on sale this very day. He wanted desperately to be in the audience. I was to go to the telephone booth in the corridor (no mobile phones then) and keep trying until I could get through to the Box Office. He said I would have to be patient – the number would be very busy and it could take a long time before I got through but I was not to give up. "Peter" I said, "do you realise how important this meeting is? Your whole future is being discussed."

He knew the meeting was important but he had different priorities. After all, his life expectancy was not the normal three score years and ten. He didn't know whether he would be here from one day to the next, so in his eyes, planning for a future could be put on hold for a bit. In the event, I managed to get through to the booking office reasonably quickly and Dr. Frankel and the rest of the staff present now also had to consider how Peter could get to the concert. Peter had come home to us for the odd day's outing but this took an awful lot of planning. Firstly, he had to be lifted into the front passenger seat of our car and padded all round with pillows to stop him from slipping. His wheelchair had to be dismantled and packed into the boot of the car. We needed his brother plus another strong man to assist when we got home just to transfer him back to his wheelchair before we could even get him into the house.

In these days, he didn't have a portable suction machine but there was a local hospital that was kind enough to lend us one of theirs. The district nurses were on standby and promised to come if we were really worried and needed their help so we just about managed. A whole day's open air concert, however, was a rather more dangerous expedition although much more exciting as far as Peter was concerned.

The Live Aid concert on the 13th July 1985 at Wembley Arena was a goal to aim for and everyone did their level best to make it a success for Peter. David and his wife Sue were to accompany him but the remaining ticket had to be used for a trained member of staff to go with them in case Peter experienced problems. He had so many volunteers from staff willing to give up their day off to go to the concert! This first Live Aid concert has gone down in history as a massive fund raising event organised by Bob Geldof and his group The Boomtown Rats to help the starving people in Africa. To Peter though, it was more personal; he had proved he could take part in things once more and not be totally confined to a hospital environment.

It was time to spread his wings further. I had been to an exhibition in London full of equipment for the disabled and had seen vehicles especially adapted to transport people in wheelchairs. No more the indignity of being man-handled into the passenger seat of an ordinary car but he could travel in relative comfort in the back of a vehicle, seated in his own wheelchair. I knew he had to have one on these specialised vehicles. We tried getting funding from Motability but this was all going to take too long. Peter needed his vehicle now while he was fit enough to be able to use it and so we got the funds together ourselves. He couldn't wait to take delivery of this, his first car (really an adapted Ford Escort Estate). It would make travel so much easier for him but first the roof had to be raised and other adaptations made before he actually received it which wasn't until January 1986 and by then he had already left Stoke Mandeville.

About the same time, Julie had been told about an organisation called 'The Across Trust' through a colleague at her office. They arranged holidays for very severely disabled people by 'Jumbulance' - a purpose-built vehicle designed for the long-distance transportation of disabled and sick people. It was fitted with beds for the unable and reclining seats for helpers; almost like a mini-hospital with its own kitchen, respiratory equipment and medical supplies. There was a doctor on board, nurses and a physiotherapist plus other care attendants. All staff paid their own expenses so costs for the disabled were not prohibitive. Although it was a Roman Catholic organisation, the holidays were open to all irrespective of their religious beliefs. Julie was quite happy to give up ten days of her holiday entitlement to travel with Peter and there was a young female doctor at Stoke Mandeville also keen to go. The trip suggested for Peter was to

Lourdes but he took a lot of persuading before he agreed to give it a go. For a start, he said he was not a devout Christian and he knew there would be no miracle cure for him. He didn't know if he could stand the long journey just to visit a religious shrine but as Julie said "just look on it as a holiday in the South of France at a very cheap price for that region".

As it happened, both he and Julie had a wonderful time. True, there was no miraculous cure, in spite of visiting the Shrine of our Lady, the Grotto and taking part several times in the Candlelit procession which is a regular awe-inspiring event once darkness falls but then Peter didn't expect a miracle. I know, however, he would agree when I say in some ways, there was something very special about this trip. He gained inner peace from the visit and was most impressed by the place, particularly the candlelit procession each day. Kathy, the young doctor and Julie got on extremely well together and although they were very tired from all their exertions by the end of the 'holiday', they both wanted to do another trip the following year.

Now, his time at Stoke Mandeville couldn't be extended any further. He had been there longer than most and he had to move on. He was not ready for independent living and there were very few places able to accommodate him. When the Royal Hospital and Home for Incurables at Putney was suggested, we were all horrified. It sounded a terrible place and we didn't know what to do. Julie and David made a secret visit there and reported back with mixed feelings. Peter though was more philosophical and it was agreed that he go there on a month's trial to see how he liked it. He was adamant that he didn't want to come back to our house to live and with the benefit of hindsight, I must agree, he probably made the correct decision. We would not have been able to manage him at home and give the proper care he required. It would also have been more difficult to establish independent living for him when the time was right. Nevertheless, he had to go somewhere and there would be ongoing therapy, a good ratio of staff to patients and hopefully, training for life outside a hospital environment at Putney.

The Across Jumbulance ready for action.

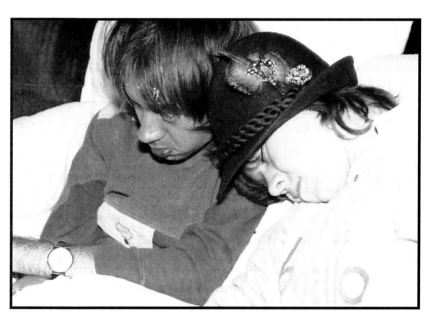

Peter and sister Julie tired on their return from Lourdes

Putney

Peter was transferred from Stoke Mandeville to The Royal Hospital and Home for Incurables in Putney at the end of September 1985. (What an awful name for a place. We kept thinking 'abandon hope all yea who enter here') One of his favourite nurses had accompanied him and completed a very thorough hand-over. We were there to meet him when he arrived and he was admitted to Drapers ward on the new Chatsworth Wing. He was given a room of his own behind the nursing station which afforded him some privacy but, as it had an opaque glass brick wall on the side nearest the main ward, it was easy for the staff to keep an eye on him. The ratio of staff to patients was extremely good and everyone did all they could to make him feel comfortable and us less uneasy about this dramatic change.

Dave immediately went about setting up an alphabet board for staff to use although obviously it would take some time for them to get familiar with Peter's special means of communication. For now, the most important thing was for staff to know how Peter expressed 'yes' and 'no'. With a list of appropriate questions, they could just about manage and hopefully he wouldn't feel too unsafe or be very uncomfortable when we were not there. We had made a rough care plan detailing how he liked to sleep, be fed, suctioned, positioned in his chair etc. Most important of all was explaining about his diaphragmatic pacemakers because of course nobody at Putney had ever seen this type of equipment before. We did not leave until nearly midnight and promised to be back early the next day. I could see by the look in Peter's eyes that he was really terrified of being left in this strange place without family or friends, but we were helpless to interfere. Thank goodness we could visit as often and for as long as we liked.

It was amazing how quickly Peter settled into his new abode. The wing was quite detached from the main hospital and the emphasis was on rehabilitation for each individual patient in so far as this was possible. They had bought a new shower trolley identical to the one Peter had used when he was at Stoke Mandeville and the nursing auxiliaries became adept at feeding and toileting him. Learning to communicate in his special way took rather longer and great patience on all sides. Doctors and senior nursing staff never really did get the hang of it due mainly I suspect, to the fact they didn't want to appear stupid in front of junior colleagues.

He missed the companionship of the other young men he had bonded with at Stoke Mandeville though. Chatsworth wing was quite small in so far as numbers of patients and sadly, most of these had some form of mental impairment. Even the most able ones couldn't conduct a conversation with Peter. We learned the history of a few through their relatives who visited and we relayed this information to Peter so he could build up a mental picture of those around him.

Christiana was injured when she had stopped to change a wheel on her car after getting a puncture on a French motorway. She had pulled on to the hard shoulder but a lorry had ploughed into her as she bent down to examine the damage to the tyre. I think she had her young children with her at the time but they were in the car and escaped injury. Her mother visited Christiana almost daily and tried to encourage her. She hadn't spoken since the accident and refused to swallow any food or liquid so was fed through a tube in her stomach. She was quite young and looked completely normal but was unable to recognise anyone, eat anything or move out of her chair. She looked so wistful; we always made time to talk to her. She appeared to listen intently, had a lovely smile but gave no real response to anything said to her.

Paul was a young lad involved in a car accident. He had been an apprentice at one of the large car manufacturers and had gone to visit another apprentice who was off sick at the time. Paul's injuries only appeared slight at the time of the accident but before he could be sent home from the Accident and Emergency department, he collapsed with a clot on his brain. He too appeared in a semi-comatose state unable to communicate or do anything for himself.   His parents were very regular visitors. He was very fond of our daughter Julie, who was about the same age as himself, and she was able to evoke some response from him when she chatted even though he was unable to answer her questions except by smiling if she got something right.

One young man had long poles fixed to his wheelchair to prevent him getting through the door and out of the ward. If he was provoked in any way, he could be violent to other patients, staff or visitors. We rarely saw anyone visit him and so we were unable to ascertain what had happened to cause his condition and mental state. Most of the other patients were in similar situations or worse. Many suffered epileptic fits due to their brain injuries but fortunately, Peter was never troubled in this way. In fact it was at about this time that he queried why he had to take medication to prevent an epileptic fit. As he pointed out, he had not had a fit so far and he had heard that the medication prescribed as a prophylactic measure had side effects and could have a detrimental effect on his teeth. Rather late in the day I'm afraid as some damage had already been done to his teeth but at least he could stop a further deterioration in this area.

There was also an older gentleman on Peter's ward who was probably in his early fifties. He came from the Newmarket area and had been a racehorse trainer when he was younger until he unfortunately suffered quite a severe stroke. His speech was now hardly coherent and he couldn't stand without support. Nevertheless he could propel himself in his wheelchair and transfer to another seat or bed when the occasion demanded this. His main aim in life was to get away from Putney and back to Newmarket, training or at the very least watching his beloved horses. Of course he was not in a fit state to do this but he never gave up trying. He would ask any person he thought likely to listen and accede to his request, to telephone for a taxi for him. Usually the ward staff were aware of his intentions and able to thwart his attempts. However occasionally, he managed to find someone who was unaware of his limited capabilities and prepared to call a taxi for him. He would wait by the front door of the hospital in the hope he could escape before his absence was noticed by the ward staff. I remember once he did manage to get a cab driver to take him to the railway station where he boarded a train for Newmarket. He was not found until the following day when he arrived at the Newmarket race track. He had spent the night in a hotel, after miraculously persuading the manager to help him to bed. Somehow he then managed to get himself to the races the next morning. Philosophically, Peter said at least he had enjoyed his taste of freedom while it lasted.

Peter too had a taste of freedom not too long after he arrived at Putney as he had already booked another holiday with the Across organisation. Julie and the young doctor, Cathy, were again in the party but this time they travelled to Rome and Austria and had the opportunity to meet Pope John Paul who gave each of them an individual blessing. I know he enjoyed the break from the mundane routine of hospital life and the company of his fellow travellers.

As often as possible, Peter liked to get out in the grounds of the hospital where the paths were wheelchair friendly and he could escape the monotony of life on the ward. He did have his alarm in the head rest of his chair, and providing he didn't spasm too badly, he could summon assistance if he needed help. He also made firm friendships, mainly with nursing auxiliaries who saw to his daily care. They kept him in touch with the outside world and told him all about their personal lives, seeking his advice and opinion on a variety of issues. I think because Peter couldn't speak, they always felt their secrets were safe with him. He was a good listener and it pleased him to be involved.

There was one particular young lady of Afro-Caribbean descent who would have liked to look after Peter completely on her own without the interference of anybody else. Whilst she probably was better than most at feeding and tending his needs, she did upset the other girls by telling them what to do and how to do it. Her friendship with Peter progressed and gradually, she spent more and more time with him, both on and off duty, until the ward sister, worried about possible repercussions of this liaison, tried to put a stop to it. She felt it inappropriate for Ulla to spend so much time with Peter and altered the rota so she no longer looked after him when she was working. She even tried to ban her visiting him in her own time and naturally, they were both very cross about this. Peter felt he had rights and he would not be dictated to about his personal life. He would not be told who he could and could not see or what was appropriate or otherwise for his well-being. He felt it was bad enough that he had to have every thing done for him just to stay alive but he was adamant he was not allowing anyone to take over control of his life. He refused to be got out of bed, or to eat or drink anything until there was a proper enquiry and the matter resolved. He insisted the senior nursing officer be called so he could state his case. He said he was not a child, would choose his own friends and make his own decisions about how he lived his life. Eventually the senior nursing officer arrived and listened to the whole story although this wasn't easy. Neither she nor the ward sister could communicate directly with Peter and everything had to be discussed via a third party and guess who this was? Ulla. A compromise was reached. She would be allowed to work with Peter again but not interfere when other auxiliaries were caring for him and she could visit in her own time providing he was not undergoing treatment or care.

We will always be grateful to Ulla though. Our son felt safe when she was around and if there was a problem, she would always let us know so we could deal with it. The real bonus was the fact she wanted to get Peter more involved in the outside world. They discussed everything under the sun from food to fashion, McDonalds to the music scene. She took him to the local shops, helped him choose his clothes and came home with him on her weekends off duty. I think she had never had much family life of her own and she enjoyed participating in ours. Usually, it was just for the day but on several occasions she spent the whole weekend with us. Dave would collect them in Peter's car which had now been delivered to him at Putney and I would alert our own district nurses just in case they were needed. How we managed to man-handle Peter upstairs to sleep in his old bed at night, was nothing short of a miracle. Why didn't we arrange a bed downstairs for him? I don't think it occurred to us or to him for that matter.

Peter was given a special parking space at the Royal Hospital & Home for his car when he finally took delivery. I think he used to keep an eye on it himself during the week, he was so proud of his Chairman Escort. I know he looked forward to being able to go for a drive without quite so much hassle whenever one of his visitors felt able to take him. He had it fully insured for any driver but of course there were only a few people willing and able to look after Peter away from the safe environment of the hospital. If Ulla wasn't working, she would happily go along with him on his outings although she didn't drive herself. Still, at least this meant that his driver didn't have to worry too much about what was happening in the back of the car with Ulla by his side. Peter loved to go out to the nearby Richmond Park to watch the deer or best of all to a pop concert at Wembley, Earls Court or a similar venue. I well remember the first time his cousin Debbie was taking him to one of these events with her in the driving seat. She was so anxious not to do anything wrong and concentrating so hard on giving Peter a smooth ride, she forgot completely about the 'sleeping policemen' (speed humps) across the driveway at the hospital. She was mortified when Peter nearly joined her in the driving seat as he shot out of his chair but he wasn't too bothered – said he just needed readjusting to a more comfortable sitting position before they could proceed. Anyway, he said the concert was well worth a little inconvenience.

I am not so sure he felt the same about his visit to Sadler's Wells. I can't even remember exactly when it took place but I know who accompanied him on this occasion. The outing was arranged as a special Christmas present for my mother who was very fond of ballet even though she had never actually managed to see a live performance at one of the famous London venues. It was always difficult to know what to give her for her birthday or Christmas so Julie suggested to Peter they could treat their Nan, as a surprise and take her to see The Nutcracker Suite which was being shown at Sadler's Wells. In a mad moment he agreed although to say he wasn't exactly a fan of ballet himself, was rather an understatement. The box office arranged really good seats for Julie and my mother together with a wheelchair space for Peter, right at the front of the theatre. After only a very short time, I think Peter realised his mistake as Julie did too if the truth be told, but both for different reasons. It was warm in the theatre; he was bored and fell asleep. This made his pacemakers very noisy; the sound of his heavy breathing echoing round the stalls for all to hear with the exception of my mother who was quite deaf on the side nearest to him. She was entranced with the performance on stage but Julie couldn't bear to watch and cringed with embarrassment. In spite of all her efforts, she was unable to stop the noise coming from her brother who was oblivious to the disruption he was causing. In future, he said he would only go to things he knew he liked. He didn't mind treating his Nan to the theatre but she would have to do without his company if she wanted to go to the ballet again.

It was relatively easy to book suitable seats at most theatres or event venues for Peter. Most places had special seating arrangements for the wheelchair bound at discounted rates and sometimes there was a free ticket for one carer. Of course, Peter really had to have two people with him but it could usually be arranged for them to all sit together. I only ever remember there being a problem on one occasion with some pop star. When he made his entrance on stage, the audience stood up and Peter was unable to see very much at all. However, this was at the Royal Festival Hall and the manager was most apologetic. He more than compensated for Peter's loss of enjoyment by giving him complimentary tickets for himself plus two carers at another concert of his choosing.

Not long after his arrival at Putney, Peter was to be presented with the gold medal by the Girdlers' Company as recommended by Stoke Mandeville. The Royal Hospital & Home at Putney, although Peter was funded by the NHS, was really a private hospital and they saw this as a good Public Relations opportunity. The Governors were coming to the presentation as were members of staff from Stoke Mandeville and of course our friends and family. We arranged a lunch afterwards in the beautiful Wedgwood Hall for all the visitors. Up until now, we had all completely shunned publicity but now we were so proud of our son it seemed the right time to talk to the press. Dave contacted the London Thames television news team and also gave information to the 'Today' newspaper. He knew the editor of this daily paper as she had previously been the publisher of magazines he worked on. He was confident she would see their reporter got the story right and only print after seeking Dave's approval.

I remember the reporter Thames News sent to cover the story was a young man by the name of Paul Larsmon and we always think of the sensitive manner in which he handled the interviews with Peter and the family, whenever we see him on television today.   As a result of the publicity, Peter did gain some benefits.   A computer scientist at Bristol University introduced him to the speech synthesiser he had invented. This was a portable machine with pre-recorded sentences and basic phrases. It had rechargeable batteries and could be accessed by means of a mouth stick. Also, another computer expert with a consultancy business in Merseyside contacted us with a view to helping Peter.   He had adapted a Macintosh computer to make it suitable for use by severely disabled people. Instead of using a conventional keyboard, access was achieved by wearing a special headset and attached mouthpiece. Slight movement of the head – up or down or from side to side would move the cursor around the screen and blowing or sucking on the mouthpiece could operate a switch.   Due to the generosity of a scaffold company in the north of England, the cost of £6,000 would be covered and Peter would be receiving the equipment completely free of charge. Unfortunately, Putney did not have skilled occupational therapists available for the amount of time needed to work with Peter to utilise all this highly technical machinery and realise its full potential in spite of his extremely limited movement.   Access was still the greatest problem. He could not control his slight head movement sufficiently and maintain a position for long enough for this method of access to be effective and he could only be patient for so long. The weather was getting warmer and he did like to be able to spend as much time away from the ward as possible.

Hiccups

All the outside activities did contribute to some trouble with Peter's skin. He had always been fairly lucky in this regard partly due to the fact that he had more or less full sensation. This meant that he knew when he was uncomfortable in his chair and could get someone to shift his position so alleviating any skin problems before they had a chance to start. It is usually sitting in the same position for a long time without respite that causes the skin to become inflamed and break down. However, it could simply be an unwanted crease in the back of trousers or an unnoticed crumb that caused an irritation and before very long at all a sore developed. The only treatment in this situation is to stay off the area until it heals completely and this can take a very long time. In Stoke Mandeville the remedy used to be a sort of flat trolley which could be used instead of a wheelchair by the patient, who could then lie on their stomach. If they were able to propel themselves, they could get around quite quickly although of course their view of the world was restricted to a very low level. This was not possible for Peter however, when he developed a sore. He could not lie on his stomach because of his tracheotomy and his method of breathing. He had no option but to try bed rest. Progress was very slow, not helped by the fact that he hated being confined to bed and insisted on getting up, if only for a short time, most days. The sore was right at the base of his spine over the coccyx. Eventually, a consultant surgeon was brought in to give his opinion on the problem and he was told the best option would be an operation. The surgeon could shave a bit off the bone causing the trouble and then cover the site with a swing graft. Peter would still have to stay in bed after the operation but only for a relatively short time instead of the months that could be involved. He couldn't wait for the operation to be done so he could get on with his life. Fortunately, it was very successful and soon Peter was back at Putney again to recuperate. All this did make us think about his car though. The Chairman Escort was originally only a van and the springing was nowhere near as good as it would be in a saloon car. Another patient at Putney had a Nissan Prairie Car which had been adapted so his wheelchair could go in the back similar to Peter's but affording much more comfort to its occupant. Peter had a test ride in it and his mind was made up. He needed to change his car in the not too distant future.

The risk of a chest infection was always present because of Peter's breathing problems and if antibiotics weren't administered at the first sign of trouble, (usually a slight temperature and bit of sweating) he could become confused and dangerously ill very quickly. After he had been at Putney for almost a year, I visited him as usual one afternoon and was most alarmed to see him in bed looking quite flushed. Worst of all, he didn't seem to be able to concentrate sufficiently to spell out anything that made sense. I asked for the doctor to be called straight away and on his examination an ambulance was immediately summoned. Peter was being taken at high speed to Phipps Respiratory Unit with me following behind in my car, not sure exactly where he was going or whether he would survive the trip. I wondered if his father and I would be able to get to see him alive again. This unit was housed in the South Western Hospital but was really a part of St. Thomas' in London and probably the best in the country for breathing problems. It was the start of a long association with the Respiratory Unit of St. Thomas' hospital.

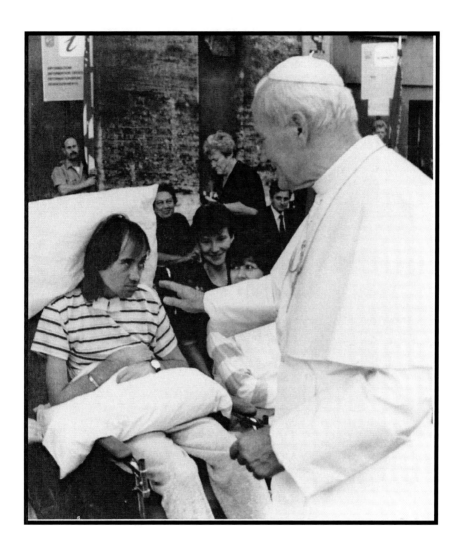

Peter being blessed by Pope John Paul in Rome.

Receiving his Gold Medal from the Master of the Girdlers Company,
Captain G.M.A. James

Grounds at Putney where Peter liked to sit.

Phipps Unit

We all owe so much to the care and devotion of the highly trained and experienced medical, nursing and technical staff who worked on the Respiratory Unit which was housed on the Phipps Unit of the South Western Hospital, Stockton, although was really under the auspices of St. Thomas' Hospital, Westminster in London. It was due to the skill and tender loving care of these people that Peter's life was saved on several occasions over the ensuing years.

On this, his first admission, life on the Phipps Unit passed in a daze for Peter. I don't think any of us realised that such a place existed or that there were so many different types of machinery to assist people with breathing difficulties, the majority of which were as a result of contracting polio earlier on. We did not know that iron lungs were still used and had never even heard of a cuirass or a rocking bed for example. The rocking bed reminded us of a see-saw but was quite spectacular in operation. The lady being nursed on one of these beds went rhythmically up and down for several hours to improve her breathing. The theory is that when you are in an upright position, the lungs expand and if you stand on your head, air will be pushed out of your lungs. Apparently it takes a long time to get used to the see-saw action of the rocking bed which can cause dizziness or nausea. Most of the machinery relied on electricity for its operation and it was vital, therefore, for a good back up generator in case of power failure.

The consultant in charge, Dr. Spencer, always seemed to be around. He would do anything possible to assist with the well being of his patients, maintaining their dignity and independence and treating them almost like paying guests in a five star establishment even though the building itself was far from perfect, to put it kindly. Patients own ideas about what needed to be done to improve their state of health were seriously considered and acted upon if at all practical. In spite of their extremely severe physical disabilities, the majority of these people lived in their own homes albeit with an awful lot of care. If they did have to come into hospital for a spell, either as an emergency with a chest infection or a planned admission for surgery or another form of treatment, their carers were catered for as well. They were treated as part of the team looking after the patient, not just a visitor but a respected professional. They were given their own room and made welcome to use the staff facilities, canteen etc. In the nineteen eighties, this was most unusual and it gave us all different ideas about the way forward for Peter. Maybe, one day he would be able to live in his own home again. We would definitely like to investigate the possibility.

Dr. Spencer was well supported by truly dedicated staff and nothing was too much trouble for any of these people. The senior nursing officer, M/s Gill, was a lovely lass from the North of England, very down to earth and approachable with an excellent team of nurses and auxiliaries under her command. However, it was not just the medical and nursing staff that made this place such a centre of excellence. Technicians, radiologists, auxiliaries and cleaning staff all played their part in putting the welfare of the patients before anything else. The fact that the unit was in such antiquated premises hardly seemed to matter. Each patient had space for their equipment around their own bed and visitors were welcome at any time. The atmosphere was friendly and homely in spite of the grave state of health of most of the patients.

As soon as he was well enough to be aware of his surroundings and the other patients, he was full of questions about how they all managed and could live at home. The lady opposite Peter was named Heather and she was a real inspiration to him. She had contracted polio as a child and now had to spend the majority of her time encased in an iron lung. Whenever she developed a severe chest infection, the big ambulance which was attached to the unit, would go out to her home near Colchester in Essex and bring her to the unit for admittance and emergency treatment. She arrived in her own iron lung, which was painted a delicate shade of pink, with her two Danish carers and all the paraphernalia required to help make her stay as comfortable as possible. This always included a heated towel rail and her own soft towels and toiletries. She had a mirror fixed in the lid of the iron lung which meant she could see Peter in the bed opposite and she took a great interest in him. The Danish carers would be sent back and forth to Peter with questions and answers and then when we visited, she would quiz us in more detail and also fill us in on the events of the day, his progress etc. Heather was a remarkable lady, who in spite of her severe disabilities did so many things. She had her own adapted bungalow and a car and liked to go out as often as possible. She was a fine artist, painting with a brush in her mouth. She felt herself lucky to be given work by the charity supporting foot and mouth artists. She encouraged us all to think that one day, Peter would be able to live in his own home again, maybe with the help of Danish carers like hers - but she could at least tell them what she wanted done and Peter couldn't even make a sound, let alone speak. Still, it was nice to dream. Meanwhile, for the time being, he would have to return to Putney, although we promised ourselves we would see what possibilities there were for someone like Peter.

We went to see the Senior Nursing Officer of the Unit (M/s Gill) in her cupboard sized office attached to the ward. I think she was half expecting us and all our questions about how Peter could live in his own home. She told us we would have to be very patient and prepared for a long battle before we had a hope of getting the necessary funding for the venture, let alone somewhere suitable for our son to live or carers to look after him. Nevertheless, she felt our aspirations could be achieved if this is what Peter wanted and we were all prepared for the hard work to come. We couldn't wait to get started.

For the present, after about ten days, he was well enough to be discharged back to Putney. Beds on the Phipps Unit were in great demand for people who required urgent treatment for serious respiratory problems. Peter's chest infection had been cleared for the present and his condition stabilised although it was necessary for him to be admitted again on a couple more occasions before the new unit at St. Thomas' hospital itself was built.

Dr. Geoffrey Spencer - Consultant

Celia Gill – Senior Nurse Manager

Return to Putney

To get back to basics, during his first year at Putney, considerable efforts were made to provide Peter with a suitable and comfortable NHS wheelchair, electric or manual, but without success I'm afraid. He needed a chair with a head rest that actually supported his head, a back rest that could be tilted to change his position and cradles for his arms which could hopefully be adapted to take a support for a piece of equipment when necessary. The only part that was right was the Roho cushion which he sat on in the chair. This had been adapted so as to protect the area where the skin graft had been done previously over his coccyx.

I remember after more and more adjustments to the wheelchair to try and improve the situation, Peter confided to me he would like to push the whole contraption over London Bridge. To be fair, his needs were specialised, funding was limited and the staff were trying to adapt off the peg models instead of having something tailor made for him. For the time being, he would continue to use his privately purchased electric chair.

Peter was a past master at getting his own way. For instance, the hospital had changed the way they provided meals for their patients and he did not approve at all. The food was all pre-cooked now and stored ready to be brought 'back to life' as Peter termed it, when required. I must admit it wasn't as appetising as the previous method when fresh ingredients were cooked in their own kitchens and served the same day, but hygiene was given as the reason for the change. He said he was unable to swallow the food for various reasons. I remember being instructed by him to take his plate of food to the Senior Nursing Officer on several occasions to explain why it was inedible so far as he was concerned. In the end, he was given a budget and allowed to choose dinners from the local freezer centre which he said caused him no problem at all. They could be defrosted and cooked in the ward's microwave as and when required and did not contravene their health and hygiene policy. Fresh fruit and other delicacies to supplement his diet, which he could manage to eat without difficulty, were supplied to him by the hospital.

On one occasion, Peter had planned a party for a special celebration. He had invited family and friends and intended holding it in a community area which he knew he could use without permission. However, when the date drew near it became obvious he was not going to be able to leave his bed because of problems with his skin. He didn't mind going to his party in his bed but this would not go through the doors of the proposed venue. He knew of another suitable room with very wide doors, but patients were not usually allowed to use this place. However he thought if his dad asked the Nursing Officer, permission would be granted for him to host his party there. He was right. She thought that Dave was connected with the press in some way and didn't want to court any bad publicity. Naturally we didn't explain he actually worked on the **advertisement** side of the **gardening** press and as such was not really able to influence daily newspaper editors as to the content of their publications. She remembered he had arranged for the media to be present at the Award ceremony some time earlier and didn't want to take any chances. I am afraid that Peter used this ruse on several other occasions when he wanted a favour or special consideration, during the rest of his stay at the RHHI.

There was one particular family who were exceptionally good to Peter during the time he spent at Putney. Both Haley and her mother worked there as auxiliaries and they treated him as a normal person who did not have any problems. They invited him to their home and often accompanied him to any special events going on at the hospital so he wouldn't miss out. The whole family had the right approach to disability and did all they could to make Peter feel wanted and worthy of their attention. He certainly needed all the friends possible when he was moved from the well staffed and therapy motivated enclaves of Drapers Ward to a so-called 'self care' ward.

The move came without much prior warning and our protests that it wasn't suitable for him fell on deaf ears. The 'powers that be' had decided it was time for Peter to move on if he was serious about his desire to move back into the community and there was nothing we could do about it. He was given his own room but the staff ratio was much lower and therapy very limited. He couldn't even have a shower every day and was told he would have to make do with just twice a week as the members of staff here were far too busy to shower him every day

One thing he would not give way over was his meals. He was supposed to eat in the dining room attached to self-care. It was a laborious task feeding Peter at any time, as he had such difficulty in chewing and swallowing but food was one of his greatest pleasures; he liked an unhurried meal and social chit-chat whilst he dined and was determined feeding would be done properly. If he ate in the dining room, the one feeding him had other things to distract them. This resulted either in him being made in a mess because of insufficient attention to the job in hand, or the food was rammed into his mouth so quickly it caused a coughing fit. No, Peter insisted if he was going to eat at all, he had to have his meals in his own room. I am afraid some of the auxiliary members of staff were rather sullen about this as they much preferred to be in the company of others so they could chat and relieve the tedious task of feeding someone who took so long to eat. He would have to wait till last to be fed and consequently, the food was often unappetising because it had hung around for so long and had to be reheated. Ulla or Haley often helped out by coming over to self-care on their break, saying they would give Peter his lunch whilst they visited him. As often as we could, one of us would arrange our visit to coincide with the evening mealtime and then we took over the job.

For the first few months on this 'self-care' ward, Peter was far from his usual cheerful self. We were quite worried because he seemed to have hit a real low spot which was most unlike him. He was such a fighter and to see his spirit crushed like this was devastating. To make matters worse, they were carrying out extensive building works in the grounds of the hospital where a new brain injury unit was to be built. This curtailed Peter's access to the gardens and his only gateway to freedom, where he could pretend he was not part of the hospital community. Finally, he petitioned the powers that be in his usual manner; -a mixture of pleas, gentle blackmail and threats of dad's intervention. Temporary ramps were put in so he could get outdoors once more and his good spirits at least partially returned.

He couldn't do too much himself about looking into the possibilities of a home of his own at this stage, so he busied himself with the welfare of the other occupants of the self-care unit. There were two groups of staff here. Roughly half were recruited in the Philippines and the majority of the remainder were from one of the Caribbean Islands. These two factions did not get on together at all well and their arguments often reflected badly on their work with patients. Some of these people were paying for the privilege of being cared for in this place and yet they seemed to have no say in how they were treated or how their money was spent. Peter, as usual wanted to be their champion but of course this involved us and we really had enough of **his** battles to fight. Sometimes there were so many things to sort out when we arrived to see Peter; it was time for us to leave again and we had hardly spent any quality time with him. Always, we had to go and see his friend Michael – a man who due to very severe cerebral palsy I think, spent most of his time in what looked like an open coffin on wheels. Peter would save some special titbit for us to give to him. Michael didn't have many visitors himself and was always pleased if anyone came to his room. His arms and legs would be flaying in all directions and he never failed to tell us to get Peter out of Putney whilst he was still young. He said it wasn't a suitable place for him. Then there were always people who needed some personal problem sorted out for them and Peter had volunteered our services. This often involved yet more petitions to the senior nursing officers but what else could we do?

There was one particular gentleman patient called John who often managed to upset Peter. Poor man, he couldn't really help the way he behaved. His brain had been damaged, I think as a result of a stroke or a cerebral haemorrhage. John liked to sit in his wheelchair in the corridor, often within earshot of conversations going on around Peter's room. . He would make loud, rude comments, often of a sexual nature, about visitors or other patients. He usually wore a stained black dinner suit complete with bow tie and on his head a black bowler hat. His shirt was protected with a type of asbestos apron to prevent him setting himself alight from the cigarettes he constantly smoked. Normally Peter would ignore his sexual comments and swearing but one day when a young and pretty lady member of staff was with Peter, he could stand it no longer. He put his wheelchair into forward gear and headed straight for John, crashing into his wheelchair at top speed and almost knocking him over. For once John was dumbfounded as he tried to straighten himself up in the chair and retrieve his smouldering cigarette before Peter charged again, managing for once to get the reverse and forward gears to react quickly to his chin control commands. Then, in a very soft trembling voice, John said "that wasn't very nice Peter". The staff could hardly hide their laughter as Peter turned his wheelchair round and swept back to his room. Both wheelchairs required minor repairs but apart from that, no harm was done and John didn't taunt the females so much – at least for a week or so. I know some people manage to become good wheelchair athletes, but wrestlers? The notoriety Peter gained from this escapade made him quite a favourite with the young nursing auxiliaries though.

Peter's real dread was Crane flies commonly known as daddy long legs. When he was lying on his back in bed he always hated the thought of one these creatures landing on his tracheotomy tube and being sucked into his lungs. How awful it must be to know there is nothing you can do about such a thing happening. Totally paralysed people cannot do so many simple things we all take for granted. I don't think we ever told him about the cockroaches that every so often appeared at night. When it was dark and we were walking through the corridors on our way home these creatures were sometimes in evidence and you heard the nauseating sound of crunching underfoot if you accidentally stepped on one. Of course this contravened good hygiene but the building was old and although appropriate treatment was carried out regularly to rid the place of the infestation, the pests soon came back.

Progress was painfully slow in respect of Peter's move back into the Community. We had been advised it would be prudent not to say too much about the plan to senior staff at Putney. We didn't want him moved to an even worse ward than the self care one where he was now. He needed as much ongoing therapy as possible and in any case, we were not at all sure when or indeed if, our plans would ever come to fruition. Things were happening though. The manager of our local young disabled unit had been to see Peter with a social worker from our home area, to discuss his expectations and desires for the future. Just as importantly, they had also been to see the senior nursing officer at the Phipps Unit to find out how other patients managed in their own homes, how they recruited suitable staff and who funded their care packages. We were not dismissed as out of hand and Joan Corry (the nursing manager of our local young disabled unit) promised to discuss Peter's case with the general manager of the community services unit, Waltham Forest Health Authority. It seemed that because Peter had so many health issues, Social Services were not involved in the funding of his care at Putney which was totally paid for by our Health Authority. I needed to spend more time working on the various issues involved if Peter was to realise his ambition to return to some sort of independent lifestyle and so I decided to give up my part-time work as a medical secretary in the private sector. Peter's future was far more important.

The fight for independence

The outlook following the first meeting we had with the Local Health Authority finance department was very pessimistic. It was pointed out to us that it would cost about £50,000 per annum to provide for Peter in his own home. At that time our Health Authority paid a supplement of about £19,000 to support Peter in the RHHI. Even if they allowed him to use all of this for his care in the community, there would be a shortfall of about £30,000 and we had no idea how we could meet this. Social Services were not at all keen on becoming involved in the package although they did say they would help with providing equipment for his home, if he did ever manage to return to live in Waltham Forest. Where could we go from here to get the additional resources required?

It had been right to give up my employment. My normal working hours were now more than filled by the challenge of getting Peter back into the community. In 1987 independent living for severely disabled people was still very much in its infancy, as I soon found out from my initial research at the local library. I couldn't find anyone else in the country let alone Waltham Forest, who was as disabled as Peter but who had managed to return to their own home environment and live completely alone, away from a hospital or care home as he wanted to do. We would not have the benefit of seeing how others had coped. Some people did use a ventilator or were totally paralysed or even had difficulty with speech but Peter had all of these problems to cope with and more – he just had a brain in a locked-in body.

There was a consumer-led 'disability movement' in the U.K. which was working towards the full integration of disabled people into society at large but realisation of their plans had a very long way to go. They suggested I contact the Hampshire Centre for Independent Living as these people had produced a source book with care support ideas, and they thought I might find this helpful. What an understatement! Their book was just what I needed and gave such good advice as to how to go about realising Peter's dream of independence. I started reading it as soon as it arrived and I could hardly wait to visit Putney to share the contents with Peter. We were both so inspired by the book we didn't stop for food, drinks or anything. At least we now had an idea as to how to proceed.

The first thing we needed to do was to assess his daily care needs and make a written record of everything that needed to be done each hour of the day and night, stating how long each task took and who could carry it out. It sounds simple now but this was what we would need before we could even try to obtain funding. It was also good practice for the care cards we made for his stay in the Larkshall Unit of Chingford Hospital. This set of cards was actually the forerunner of what became his very sophisticated Care Manual used in the training of all new carers in later years - but I am racing ahead, this was early days. We included everything as far as possible from getting up to going to bed and even a turn during the night to stop his skin breaking down. We tried not to make the tasks look too onerous and included pleasurable activities but even so, many actual working hours were needed each week and what would happen when two people were required to carry out a particular task such as lifting him in or out of his wheelchair? It would take some negotiating with our Health Authority to make Peter's package work.

Meanwhile, we managed to get Peter's name added to the housing list for a council property suitable for his needs. Ideally he required a flat or bungalow with two bedrooms, space for manoeuvring his large wheelchair and situated not too far from our home so we could be on call as and when needed. If his carers were to be recruited from abroad, they would also probably need accommodation in the vicinity, for their off-duty periods. Quite a tall order but this was the easy part. At least he fulfilled the main eligibility criterion concerning previous residency. Prior to his accident, he had always lived in the borough of Waltham Forest.

The first full case conference regarding Peter's request for independent living was held locally with all the interested parties present except for the one most affected by decisions to be made – Peter himself. The conference room used by Social Services was located on the first floor; there was no lift and it was therefore, inaccessible to him although I was allowed to attend and speak on his behalf. We didn't protest about this arrangement as we wanted to get things moving as quickly as possible and we decided we wouldn't manage this if we upset the authorities so early on. However, I did ask if it was at all possible for follow up meetings to be at a venue with suitable access for wheelchairs.

At this time, it was suggested that maybe the Community Service Volunteer Scheme could be used to eke out the limited funds available for Peter's care. Also the district nursing service said they may be able to help by visiting morning and night to avoid the necessity of two carers being present for lifting purposes. Things were looking up and I felt justified in giving Peter an optimistic report when I saw him the next day.

It wasn't too long before Peter did receive offers of accommodation although nothing really appropriate for his complex needs. Nearly a year passed before a suitable flat was identified. We were most excited and could see with the adaptations being proposed, it would be the right residence for him. Admittedly, at this moment in time, it was a terrible struggle to negotiate Peter's wheelchair through the narrow passage and doorways. Never mind, we were told that adaptations of premises for the disabled were funded by a different budget to those held by Health and Social Services and the work needed would be approved without too much hassle. His kitchen and bedroom would overlook the little garden at the back and outside his front door was another nice grassed area with two beautiful mature trees, where he would be able to sit and watch the world go by. Best of all was its location, being close to both our house and the Larkshall Unit of Chingford Hospital.

A formal offer of the tenancy of 1a The Copse, Chingford, was made in May 1988 but the conditions stated 'only minor repairs were necessary and these could be carried out once he commenced occupation'. Did they include knocking down walls, building ramps etc. as 'minor repairs'? It was well over a year later before the 'repairs' were completed and the flat ready for Peter's occupancy.

Providing a flat for his staff was also difficult because Peter could only hold the tenancy of one property. If we recruited young carers from Scandinavia, who often did this type of community placement for a year as part of their education, they would not qualify for a council owned property in Waltham Forest. Eventually it was decided probably the best option would be for Peter's staff to be allocated accommodation in the nurses' home attached to Chingford Hospital.

Peter needed to make a transitional move to the Larkshall Unit for young disabled people, so he was on the spot and could take a full part in the planning of his future. Firstly though staff from Chingford had to feel confident themselves that they would be able to cope with his special needs and sophisticated equipment. They would eventually be responsible for teaching his potential care assistants how to look after him and naturally they were a bit apprehensive. Although they were au fait with people who had spinal injuries, multiple sclerosis or motor neurone disease etc., their experience did not run to ventilator dependent patients who couldn't even speak. Senior staff would need some training themselves and Phipps Unit seemed the most appropriate place for this to take place. The experts worked here and in any case, the RHHI were not very happy or enthusiastic about how things were developing. They had reservations about all sorts of issues if Peter went ahead and moved back into the community and didn't think he would survive for more than a month or so. The best plan was for Peter to be transferred to Phipps for a couple of weeks before his move to Chingford so the local professional staff could come and receive guidance and tuition from the specialists in respiratory problems.

We had applied to the Independent Living Fund for help with finance and they had agreed in principle to our request. Our family doctor had said he would take Peter on his list if he moved to The Copse and the doctor in charge of the intensive care team at Whipps Cross Hospital was made aware of Peter's condition and said she would admit him to her ward if he did have a respiratory crisis. Hurdles were gradually being overcome and definite progress was being made. We were all getting very excited but also a bit scared about what we were doing. We realised that the staff at the RHHI knew more than most about the risks we were going to take and the problems we might encounter but Peter insisted he would be much safer in his own home Please let our plan work and for Peter to be right in his assertions – not just his cavalier attitude overriding common-sense. One young man had recently returned to his home from the RHHI. Regrettably, although he was nowhere near as seriously disabled as Peter, he lived for less than a couple of months in the outside world before succumbing to an infection. We had many reservations but the dye was caste and we couldn't give in now. He might never get another chance to break free from a hospital environment and this was what Peter wanted above all else. There was no alternative; we had to try.

Larkshall Unit

Everyone had taken such trouble in the preparations preceding Peter's arrival; it was like he was being accorded celebrity status. He was given his own room just opposite the nursing station which was large enough to accommodate all his medical equipment and personal possessions, still leaving space for a work station where his computer could be set up ready for action. All the staff who hadn't previously met Peter found a reason to look in and say hello to this new occupant who had caused such a stir. Of course the whole unit was much smaller than the RHHI and this was partly the reason why everyone was so friendly and interested in the welfare of each and every patient. They were more like a big family with Joan Corry in overall charge, everyone doing their level best to improve the lives of the residents.

There was one young man around Peter's own age and similar in outlook. He had suffered a slightly less severe spinal injury owing to a swimming accident, and he too was waiting for an adapted home of his own. The two quickly became friends and it didn't take long for Andy to master the alphabet system of communicating with Peter. They spent many hours together, often supping a few beers in the large kitchen whilst Nisha, the senior nurse prepared an Indian curry just for their consumption. They liked to watch the fox cubs which they could see from the window, playing in the field only a few feet away. Often they would both remain up until quite late at night, playing music, discussing everything under the sun and planning for their now very different futures. Andy had some use of his arms and could just about fix a drink for them both. I am not sure the night staff always approved and who could blame them but Joan Corry always insisted they were young men and should be allowed to do what they wanted as far as was humanly possible. After they had been at the unit for some time, they were joined by Marianne who was disabled through illness and waiting for adaptations to her home where she tried to live independently although her parents did share the same house.

One of Peter's first visitors was the excellent Dr. Gerard Bulger who looked after all the individuals on the unit. They were immediately at ease with each other and we felt confident this man had the right approach to treating people with disabilities. He told Peter he was quite envious of all his computer equipment and couldn't wait for a demonstration so he could see exactly how he was able to operate it. As we later found out, Gerry (as Dr. Bulger became known to us) used to be a pupil at Douai Abbey School in his youth where he was greatly influenced by Wilfrid Sollom OSB – one of the monks who lived in the adjoining monastery and taught at the abbey school.

Father Wilfrid was a genius with electronic equipment and ran a workshop at the school for aspiring young radio hams, electronic inventors etc. He told us that years ago, when he was based in Cyprus whilst serving in the Armed Forces, he was actually questioned by government intelligence officers who thought he may have been spying for the enemy which of course was completely untrue. In actual fact, as we were soon to find out, he was one of the kindest people you could wish to meet with a deep and compassionate feeling for those who had need and could benefit from his special talents. Gerry said he would contact him and see if he could help in finding some sort of solution to Peter's communication problems.

It was not very long before we heard that Father Wilfrid wanted to meet our son to see for himself and consider if there was any way he could help alleviate the great effort and exertion involved when Peter wanted to do anything with his computer equipment. Gerry took him and his dad to Douai Abbey near Reading in Berkshire and introduced them both to Father Wilfrid. This was the first of many happy visits to Douai and the start of a strong friendship with this lovely man which lasted until his untimely death in August, 2003. Dr. Bulger was also very involved in the proposed project, often accompanying Peter on his visits to Douai, giving encouragement to us all and forever interested to hear what progress had been made.

Father Wilfrid soon got to grips with Peter's problems and realised the limitations of his controllable movements. He approached things from a completely different angle to all the 'experts' who had tried to help before. Instead of trying to make Peter fit a system already in use by adapting it, he decided equipment needed to be made especially for him taking into account the movement he could realistically use to any advantage. Our trips to Douai were always punctuated by Father Wilfrid having to leave us for a while every hour or so, to attend prayers. Lunch in the monks' refectory, to which we were always invited, was often a silent meal due to their strict religious regime. Nevertheless, Father Wilfrid was a jovial man with a good sense of humour, completely au fait with life outside the abbey. He was quite rotund, partly due I suspect, to his extremely sweet tooth and our visits to the abbey were always fun. On one occasion, he took us to see the school workshop where he laboured each day and introduced us to the boys carrying out experiments there. There were pictures of Peter around the walls and diagrams depicting various theories the boys had put forward as to how he could be helped to access his computer more easily.

After firstly attempting to improve Peter's communication by using his limited jaw movement to perform switching functions, Father Wilfrid abandoned this idea due to insufficient reliability of the action and interference caused by the involuntary spasms Peter suffered without any prior warning. Instead he concentrated on harnessing the more useful and reliable single eyebrow movement still available to him. This did not increase the pressure on Peter's eyes, which tended to get very sore from constant use, due of course to his lack of an automatic blink reflex. Blinking is something the majority of us do without thinking, our eyelids acting like miniature windscreen washers to keep our eyes clean and moist. However, even this limited movement Peter could only partially control. He was able to lift the one eyebrow but it had to relax again in its own time.

Nonetheless, the eyebrow switch, mounted on the arm of a pair of spectacles was eventually made for him. This adaptation provided a small roller wheel which had to be in contact with his forehead, just above the workable eyebrow. When the brow was raised, the wheel turned the switch one way and then back again as the brow relaxed. Of course this was only a one switch application but the best that Peter's limited mobility could manage with any degree of accuracy and he thought it was brilliant. The prototype was rather heavy but for the rest of his life, the eyebrow switch mounted on spectacles was the only device he could successfully use to access his sophisticated computer equipment although of course it did gradually become less clumsy and more streamlined.

As Father Wilfrid said, "at least we can hope that at the twitch of an eye-brow the new system will slightly improve the quality of his life". We will always be indebted to Father Wilfrid for his wonderful invention, the forerunner of several of the larger organisations patented versions. We know this man did many good works but to our family, he was one person who expanded Peter's capabilities and gave meaning to his life again following the accident. Thanks are also due to Dr. Gerard Bulger who gave so freely of his own time to come with us to Douai Abbey and liaise with Father Wilfrid.

Time passed very quickly for Peter whilst he was in the Larkshall Unit. He could keep an eye on the progress of the adaptations being made to his flat and think about how he would furnish it, apart from socialising with his new friends. There were consultations to be arranged for fitting of the new wheelchair which he hoped would be far more comfortable and suitable for his movement around the flat. After all, as he himself explained, there was no point in having an uncomfortable electric wheelchair which he would find difficult to negotiate in a small space when he would be having his own carers/personal assistants who could do a far better job of pushing him wherever he wanted to go and with less damage to his own new furniture and fittings. The only time an electric wheelchair would be useful to him would be if he was out in the street and at that time, the NHS wheelchair service, strange as it seems, did not allow their chairs to be used outdoors. Jackie, the Occupational Therapist was a very practical lady and she instinctively knew what would be right for Peter and advised him accordingly.

Another very devoted lady was Mara, who looked after him in the excellent physiotherapy department located in Chingford Hospital. She had managed to acquire an electrically operated standing frame primarily for his use. Once Peter was strapped to this, he could be winched up to a fully upright position so he felt he was taking the weight of his body on his own two feet – a most important exercise for a totally paralysed person but the procedure had to be carried out very gradually or otherwise he would become extremely dizzy and nauseous. Once he took up residence in his own home, he would be able to return once a week to continue physiotherapy with Mara. Seeing him strapped in the standing frame for the first time, gave me some pleasure. I realised he could still look down on his mum; he hadn't shrunk, was still six foot tall and I was only five foot nothing. I think he too liked the sensation of being able to view his surroundings from this position.

Budgets had to be prepared for when he returned to the community. He would be expected to make some contribution out of his social service payments towards his care package and although most of his medical and surgical needs would be met by the N.H.S. there were certain items he required which they could not fund. For instance, his lung pacemaker system operated on non-rechargeable batteries and he would be expected to buy them himself at a cost of roughly £5 per week. I wrote to Duracell U.K. explaining Peter's situation and asked if we could make a wholesale purchase to cut costs. They were brilliant and said they had never heard of a story like Peter's before. They were going to support him and provide the batteries he required courtesy of their charity funds. For the remainder of his life, every six months he received a new supply direct from Duracell. Peter regularly wrote and thanked them for their kindness giving them an update on his progress.

At last the time came to advertise for carers. Originally this was done under the umbrella of St. Thomas' Hospital so we could utilise their expertise in recruiting and employing suitable job applicants who would be working solely in a disabled person's own home rather than in a hospital environment. Our local authority didn't have experience of this but as soon as they felt competent, they became the administrators and responsible for the day to day running of Peter's work force. Joan Corry took on the additional role of line manager for his staff and Peter and I were part of the interview panel after applicants were short listed for a vacancy.

In the first instance, our advertisement was worded by St. Thomas' Hospital administrators but this used the term

'Responaut Attendants' and we weren't even sure what this really meant ourselves. Later, we always advertised for 'Carers/Personal Assistants' which we felt better reflected our requirements. The job would be daunting enough for those responding without unnecessary complications.

We were very lucky because two girls who worked at Chingford Hospital expressed their interest in becoming full time carers for Peter. They would not need too much training and were already familiar with his method of communication. They were to be joined by a Danish girl and accommodation for her provided in the Nurses Home, within walking distance of his flat.

The financial side of Peter's care package was just about adequate now that the Independent Living Fund allowance had been agreed. In these early days although national insurance contributions and some other expenses were included in the budget, I am afraid there was no provision for staff holiday entitlement and statutory sick payments. Somehow we managed to muddle through with the occasional help of respite care in the Larkshall Unit. At least if it was necessary for Peter to be an inpatient, training of new carers could take place here without cost to him. Gradually we gained more experience, learning to plan properly, present a budget and obtain sufficient finance for our needs. Everyone desperately wanted the package to succeed. Waltham

Forest Health Authority were really forerunners in the field of funding independent living for someone as disabled as Peter. If his scheme worked, there would be many other authorities willing to take up the challenge.

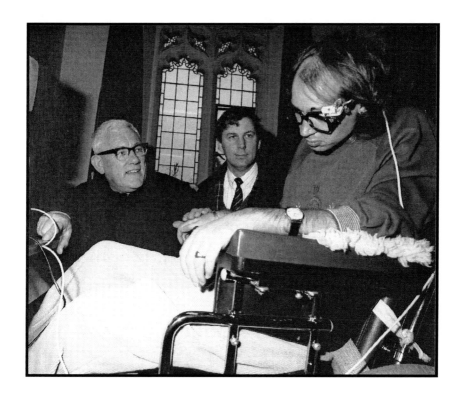

**Peter with Father Wilfrid and
Doctor Gerard Bulger.**

Working session at Douai Abbey

Early version of spectacles designed by Father Wilfrid.

Wheel just above left lens fitted tightly to Peter's eyebrow.

Front of Peter's flat in The Copse

Beautiful Copper Beech Tree in foreground.

Beginnings of true independence

At last the day had come and Peter moved into 1a The Copse. His care package was in place although we were a bit concerned about whether the inexperienced Danish girl would be able to cope. Both Laura and Lisa had been used to working with young disabled people, having served their time on the Larkshall Unit. In fact they knew Peter well and his system of communication whereas the Danish girl (let's call her Miss M) had only met him once before she started her training. However, she was very eager to work for Peter and we had reasonable reports of her progress whilst she was training. Peter was very anxious to move into his own flat and all the girls would be well supported. District nurses were coming in morning and night to help get Peter up and put him to bed. We were very local and I could be there within a few minutes if there was a problem.

That was part of the trouble though. The girls depended very heavily on our support and input on a daily basis. I was running two homes, often acting as unpaid carer for Peter for several hours each day. I do not blame the girls really for their frequent complaints. Peter was so reliant on assistance for every part of his life and the job was extremely demanding. Just coping with his communication system was intense enough and required someone's full attention without considering other aspects of the work. His personal hygiene requirements took quite a time each day apart from the mundane chores such as cooking, housework, washing and ironing which all had to be fitted in whilst they were working their shift. On the other hand, he had waited a long time for his chance to return to independence and he wanted to take part in everything. Just deciding what ingredients were required for a curry or which programmes to watch on television took up an alarming amount of time, especially when he changed his mind half way through his deliberations. Composing a shopping list each day meant there was no time left to actually **visit** the shops so I got into the habit of collecting his list in the morning and going to the supermarket for him. For the girls it must have been very frustrating and tiring. Communicating with Peter for an hour or two at a time was exhausting enough but his carer was with him for three days straight off before the shift changed! This was to give them a long break so they could enjoy mini holidays every week but it didn't benefit Peter.

We hadn't properly considered the question of sick leave and how we would cope. I think Miss M was the worst culprit. In spite of her proclamations when she applied for the job that she was "extremely fit and healthy and never ill in any way" she suffered from numerous complaints once she started working for Peter. Every time she was off sick, it meant one of the others had to stand in for her and if they couldn't oblige, it had to be me or at the weekends, Dave. Julie and David could see their dad and me getting more and more worn-out. They were full of ideas about how we should handle the situation. One Sunday morning, Dave and I had planned a rare outing. Miss M true to form rang our house and said she wasn't very well. She had a headache and would have to go home. Julie and David said **they** would handle things their way this time. Off they set for 1a The Copse. Julie told Miss M to take a couple of Paracetamol and have a sleep on the bed in her room there. Meanwhile, she promised to look after Peter until Miss M felt better and able to cope again. This wasn't what the young lady wanted at all but Julie insisted and left her no option but to comply. A couple of hours later, Julie thought she would see how the invalid was faring. Imagine her surprise when she knocked on the door and went into the girls' bedroom. There was no sign of Miss M or indeed her pot plant. The window was open and the curtain fluttering in the breeze. She had obviously decided enough was enough and had quit without facing any of us. With her pot plant under one arm, she had climbed out of the window and made off down the road. We never saw her again but Peter wasn't too unhappy about this just saying he wouldn't have to listen to her awful choice of music or face her cooking ever again.

Only trouble was this forced us to advertise once more for staff. Recruitment was a big drain on funds, not just because of the cost of the actual advertisement but training took a long time even when a suitable applicant had been found and that person couldn't be expected to work for nothing whilst she was learning the job. Two or three times Peter had to return to the Larkshall Unit because of a problem with carers or rather the lack of them.

Eventually we changed the pattern of the rota so the girls only worked for one 24 hours session at a time before they had a break and even this included a sleep over. Consequently, they were less tired when finishing a shift although their working week was spread over more days and of course they couldn't enjoy little holidays on a weekly basis as they did previously. In later years, we adjusted the pattern of the working day again, delaying the start and finishing time until 10.30 a.m. each morning. This meant Peter would already be washed and up in his chair before the previous day's carer went home. If someone did ring in to report sick, at least I could take over if he was already up and then I had the rest of the day to find another carer willing to do an extra overnight. Happy days!

One thing that never failed to amaze me was how Peter managed to remember the complete contents of his refrigerator, freezer and store cupboard and knew instinctively what needed replacing. No wonder he insisted on seeing everything before it was put away. Yet another time consuming chore for his carers but one that made him feel in control. He decided very early on that **he** also had to have a routine and he stuck to this whenever possible. He liked to be up well before 10 am and preferred not to retire until after 10 pm at night. This wasn't always possible whilst he was reliant on district nurses coming into his home to assist with lifting him in or out of bed.

It was rather strange that Peter always had female carers although I think there were several reasons for this. There were never many male applicants for the job when we advertised. Maybe the work did not appeal to them or pay well enough but anyway, Peter himself was not displeased by this as he did like pretty young ladies looking after him. Only on two occasions was a male applicant appointed and neither of them completed their training, both citing personal reasons for their departure. I think Peter also liked the general chit chat of young women. They nearly all felt they could confide in him and tell him about the highs and lows of their lives away from work.

Peter was short of two carers when the Dobelle Institute in New York contacted him saying they needed to assess his diaphragmatic lung pacemaker system. They wanted him to travel to their laboratories in the U.S.A. for this to be done. Peter thought this would be a marvellous opportunity to have a mini holiday in the United States once the Institute had finished all their tests. Dobelle would provide accommodation for him and carers whilst the tests were carried out over a three day period but he reasoned it would be viable to fit in a few extra days sightseeing before he returned home. He would have suitable transport and just needed somewhere to stay and carers to look after him. Quite a tall order though, especially as at that time he didn't even have a full quota of staff trained to work with him in **this** country. I could just visualise how the next round of interviews would pan out; 'You will have a few weeks training and then, would you mind accompanying Peter on a trip, flying to the U.S.A. visiting a prestigious medical institute, interpreting for him whilst their staff carry out tests on his lungs and finally, driving a large vehicle around New York with Peter in the back, on a sightseeing trip?' Could we even mention any of this at an interview?

As it happened, one of the next batches of interviewees included Karen who we employed and she stayed working for Peter until the day he died. When we first met her, she had never been abroad before and hadn't even got a passport but the thoughts of foreign travel appealed to her and she couldn't wait to start her training.

Sharon was sent to us by a nursing agency and she was also happy to accompany him on the proposed trip. I remember that before we took her on, we were concerned as to whether her time with Peter would only be brief as was usual with agency staff. Would it be worth all the training involved for someone who at best would only stay a few months? Ironical really, because in the event, Sharon also stayed the course and only needed minimal teaching before she was able to become a proficient member of the team. She told me that prior to joining the agency, she had seen our advertisement in the press, cut it out and was on her way to a telephone box to ring and enquire about the vacancy. Unfortunately, the wind caught this small piece of paper and blew it away before she had a chance to make the call so she joined the agency instead. Previously, she had enrolled on a course to become a state registered nurse but had given up after the first year. It was many moons later when she eventually left Peter to continue with her career in nursing, this time embarking on a **degree** course. During her long spell working with Peter unfortunately she was always employed via the agency and therefore couldn't benefit from the more favourable terms and conditions offered to the other girls who had contracts and were 'permanent' rather than 'temporary' members of his staff. This was her choice though, probably because initially she didn't intended staying for so many years.

We were still one person short for the trip and in the end, our dear daughter Julie said she would go with her brother to make up the numbers. Actually, Julie was the only one prepared to drive the very large vehicle through the busy streets of New York even though I understand she did strew some poor unsuspecting stallholder's magnificent display of fruit and vegetables over the entire road in the Chinatown district of the city as she drove by. Prior to this episode, she had already demolished the side trims of the van whilst passing through a narrow section of the Brooklyn Bridge into New York.

The diaphragmatic pacemaker tests were unremarkable and I think the whole exercise was aimed at introducing an updated version of the transmitter. When Peter was asked what improvements the new transmitter afforded him, he said "well, when I light up, I can take a bigger draw on my cigarette." I am sure the medical people were appalled at his reply not even realising that he still smoked, in spite of his condition. However, that is how it was and it was some years down the line before he eventually quit the habit, in spite of all his chest problems.

Not long after this trip, Peter had to have the implants in his chest replaced. The ones in situ were giving him pain and he was compelled to resort to using the ventilator more and more frequently as the only alternative means of taking in sufficient oxygen vital in his struggle to avoid damaging chest infections. After several telephone consultations with Dobelle and checks by their European representative, he was seen by the consultant anaesthetist, Dr. Dennis Potter, at Kings College Hospital in London.

He had experience of the diaphragmatic pacemaker system and had got to know Peter whilst he was in Putney. He agreed the implants should be replaced and this was done as a day case at Kings under his direction without too much fuss. One of Peter's carers at that time was an ex-physiotherapist, Carole and she went into theatre with him in case he needed an interpreter. By 6 pm we were all on our way back to Chingford with the new implants in place.

We had a few friends and relatives who had the expertise and willingness to help out at very short notice if something went wrong with the transmitter box of his diaphragmatic pacemaker system or his pillow alarm. It was always an emergency if a wire came loose as this would necessitate re-soldering in the correct position at best, or sometimes rewiring completely, as a matter of extreme urgency. Roy, a neighbour of ours obliged on several occasions as did Steve (husband of Debbie) and also my cousin, Peter Kirby. All of these people were in full time occupations themselves but they never complained about our plea for their assistance. Another electrical wiring problem to be fixed from time to time concerned his special spectacles whereby he accessed his computer. Poor Steve was also very knowledgeable about computers, music centres, televisions etc. Sometimes, I used to feel quite guilty about the number of things he was asked to fix for Peter whilst Debbie, his long suffering wife would have to wait ages just to have a simple job done for her. He always said that he didn't like letting Peter down.

Once Peter moved into his flat, it seemed there were many specialists concerned with different aspects of his care. We could not fault the attention given to him by these people and will always be grateful to them. Also there was the flat itself which required more adaptations and alterations if Peter was to be comfortable. The night storage heaters which were originally installed to heat his home were not really suitable because he felt the cold so much. Waltham Forest Council agreed a gas boiler would provide a more efficient form of central heating and so after a very short time, the whole system was changed. In his bedroom, Social Services paid for an electric ceiling track hoist to be fitted. This was a very good investment because it meant he no longer needed the assistance of district nurses to get him up or put him to bed at the end of the day. His carers, after sufficient training, were able to manage both tasks unaided which suited everybody. Peter could get up and go to bed when he liked, not at a time determined by outside staff that had other commitments.

Now he had got his bed time routine sorted out to his liking, Peter turned his attention to other domestic matters and announced his home should include a pet. I'm afraid I tried to put him off this idea thinking of the extra work involved for the carers and wondering what would happen when he wanted to go on holiday. His first choice was a dog but even he realised this would not be terribly practical. He couldn't be left in the flat on his own even for a short time and a dog requires regular exercise outside whatever the weather or circumstances. The best he could hope for would be a cat, not a kitten but a fully trained sober and quiet moggie that would be content to sit around for most of the day, hopefully on Peter's lap whenever he wished. Karen (Peter's carer) thought the best thing would be for him to have a rescue cat from an animal sanctuary. This way there would be more chance of finding a puss whose personality could be verified and it would be on two weeks' approval. If it did not live up to expectations, the sanctuary would take it back and no harm would be done. In the event, Leonard, was a beautiful cat that turned out to be perfect for Peter. We had to have a cat flap installed in the bathroom and we insisted Leonard sleep there overnight with the door shut, to avoid him sneaking into Peter's bedroom and getting on his bed. If this did happen, there was the chance he could suffocate his master by covering his tracheotomy tube. Peter's cousin Stephen promised to come and feed the cat when the need arose due to holidays or hospital admissions. Peter's girls were also fond of Leonard except for the odd occasions when he would present them with a field mouse or bird he had caught. When this happened we usually got a frantic telephone call for Dave to make an urgent visit and deal with the poor little captive creature. Leonard was always waiting to greet Peter on his return home from an outing. He could hear the back flap of the car being lowered and would be ready to jump on his lap even before his master was properly out of the car. It was a very sad day when poor Leonard was run over and killed by a passing car. Everyone was upset, the girls were in tears and Dave had to arrange for burial in a suitable spot in the back garden. A flowering shrub was planted and from then on this was known as Leonard's plot.

It seemed barely a week went past without some agency visiting regarding suggested adaptations or work already in the pipeline which would give Peter a more comfortable lifestyle or greater independence. At about this time, he was also introduced to the Forest Wheelchair Service based at Whipps Cross Hospital. They had an extremely dedicated team of staff who finally managed to provide Peter with a wheelchair that was both comfortable and practical for his needs. Of course this took many months of consultations and fittings but eventually he had a chair with a reclining back, supporting head piece and arm rests all provided under the auspices of the N.H.S. If you purchase a wheelchair yourself, from an outside company, you automatically also become responsible for any necessary repairs. This can involve considerable expense, as Peter found to his cost with his previous private wheelchairs. Over the ensuing years he stayed under the care of the Forest

Wheelchair Service who updated his chair as and when appropriate.

His teeth also gave him trouble and pain from time to time, due to decay partly caused by the drugs he had to take in the first few years following his accident. The local dentist couldn't treat him and suggested the only option was probably to have all his teeth extracted and false ones fitted. However, dentures were not really an option for Peter because he wouldn't be able to hold them in place nor use them for eating. His dentist contacted the London Dental Hospital and he was put under the care of a Professor in orthodontics there. Over the years, Peter received such excellent treatment at this place he was able to retain all his own teeth and avoid the need for extractions for the rest of his life. Treatment was carried out whilst he stayed in his wheelchair which was possible because of the reclining back but how they managed to get his mouth open sufficiently to carry out fillings, descaling etc. was nothing short of a miracle. Peter's teeth were so small anyway because he had the habit of grinding them in his sleep. A special plate was made which had to be put in his mouth at night to try and avoid further damage being caused by his habit. Yet another job for the carers once he was in bed!

Another major and very worrying problem was Peter's eyes. Although he was having drops (artificial tears) put in at least hourly throughout the day and ointment at night, they were often very inflamed and always highly prone to infection. He only had useful vision from the one eye where the opening had already been reduced by stitching the outside corners together to try and allow him to close it. Using the other eye produced double vision which could not be corrected, so he had trained himself not to look through it. The thoughts of him losing his sight was inconceivable - it was so precious to him and he would not manage to have any degree of independence without it or even be able to use his computer and this had become an increasingly important part of his life. The problem was two fold. He didn't have an automatic blink and his good eye didn't even close properly at night. If only it did close completely when he wanted, the lid would afford a certain degree of protection against infection. He was given an appointment at the Lid Clinic at Moorfields Eye Hospital to see what they could do. The consultant there explained to us that it was not possible at this time to do anything which would give Peter an automatic blink but he could maybe help with surgery to make Peter's good eye close when he went to bed. The operation entailed inserting a gold weight in the eyelid to make it heavier. When he was lying flat in bed, the lid would automatically come down (rather like what happened with the china dolls popular some years ago). Again, this could be done as a day case and would not interfere with the so important movement of his eyebrow. I was told I would be able to go into theatre with him in case I was needed for communication and a date was scheduled for the procedure to take place.

Unfortunately, the ward sister was not aware I had been given permission to go into the operating theatre with Peter and it did take some time to sort things out before I was finally given the go ahead. The only spare sterile gown they could find was obviously meant for a giant of a man not a five foot nothing like me but there wasn't any time to waste arguing; we were holding up the operating list. I quickly pushed up the sleeves on the gown so I could at least see my hands, rolled up the legs to avoid falling flat on my face and clutching all the spare material around my middle, we went rushing down the ward, heading for the theatre. Surgery was uneventful and did help alleviate some of the inflammation and eye infections although he would always have to be careful and take all precautions to preserve his sight.

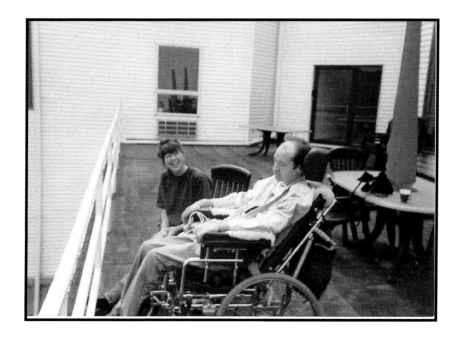

Julie and Peter at the Dobelle Institute

Peter's favourite cat - Leonard (note the cat flap)

Lane Fox Unit

The Patient Association, formed when the Phipps Unit was threatened with closure in 1968 had been extremely busy raising funds for a proposed new respiratory unit. Baroness Felicity Lane-Fox, OBE, herself a wheelchair user, made an excellent chairperson and leader of this association. With the help of patients and friends, by 1987 they had raised a million pounds and permission was given for building to commence. The unit would be housed on the same site as St. Thomas' Hospital itself and was finally opened in 1989. Sadly Baroness Lane-Fox never lived to see her tireless work come to fruition as she died in 1988. The ward was most spacious inside with fantastic views across the river Thames to the Houses of Parliament and Big Ben. All the ancillary departments required to service the unit, were catered for and even a small garden had been included for the benefit of patients who wanted to enjoy the outdoors but needed to be close to experienced staff in case of an emergency arising. The Unit was named Lane-Fox in memory of the wonderful lady who was the inspiration for raising so much cash in such a relatively short space of time. The Patients Association became Lane-Fox Respiratory Unit Patients' Association or L-FRUPA for short and it continues to raise funds to support the Unit.

The opening of Lane Fox more or less coincided with Peter's move into The Copse. It was very comforting to know that he would be able to continue under the care of such an excellent establishment whose staff would look after him if the need arose. They also operated an outreach programme and their technicians used to come to Peter's home on a regular basis to service the ventilator and portable suction machine, carrying out any necessary minor repairs on site. The transport they used when travelling to their 'clients' served a dual purpose as it could double up as an ambulance equipped to transport wheelchair passengers to and from the hospital whenever necessary. I am afraid, however, it wasn't too long before he had to test the inpatient facilities the ward offered, due to a bout of pneumonia.

It was very different here compared to the Phipps Ward although the same devoted staff members were in attendance. The place was light and airy with easy access for wheelchairs to the outside with its fabulous views across the river towards the Houses of Parliament. Beds were well spaced affording their occupants some degree of privacy in addition to room for all their equipment. If a patient had paid carers, it was now usually possible to make provision for them to be included as part of the team looking after their employer. This allowed the girls working for Peter to carry out their normal duties and shifts albeit in a different location. A small single room was allocated within the hospital buildings where they could sleep overnight. If by any chance a carer was needed to either interpret or for some other reason which couldn't wait till morning, it was now easy to arrange this. The next day the departing carer would update the one taking over from her and after passing on the bedroom door key, her shift was at an end. Peter's carers were experts at his alphabet system; they knew exactly how to make him comfortable in bed, how he liked to be fed, washed and dressed, toileted etc., and the system worked well for him. Of course it also had the advantage of freeing nurses so they could carry out their other duties. The only snag was we had to compensate carers for their fares and extra travelling time but as Peter's stay on the ward was normally only for about ten days, it was well worth while.

As soon as Peter had been admitted, x-rays and blood tests were taken so that treatment could commence. This followed the usual pattern of mainly stronger antibiotics, mechanical ventilation and deep chest physiotherapy until the infection had subsided and he could return home. His consultant, Dr. Geoffrey Spencer did not have any experience of diaphragmatic lung pacemakers and was a little dubious about their efficiency in providing enough oxygen as opposed to a ventilator. However, he always respected Peter's wishes over the matter and allowed him to return to his pacemakers once his breathing had improved sufficiently. In the end I think he did modify his opinion of the system and agreed it was suitable for Peter providing he had a back-up ventilator at home ready for use in the case of an emergency.

There were several more occasions over the following years when Peter was admitted to the Lane Fox Unit at his own request, for emergency treatment. Later Dr. Spencer retired from St. Thomas' Hospital and concentrated on the home he had established at Netley near Southampton where ventilator dependent patients and indeed their families, could enjoy a week or two's holiday knowing their medical needs would be adequately met by staff experienced in their particular problems. A bronze bust of Dr. Spencer is on a pedestal in the reception area of the Lane Fox Unit which continues to go from strength to strength now under the direction of Craig Davidson, MA MD FRCP the lead clinician for respiratory medicine and Adrian Williams, MD FRCP director of respiratory and sleep medicine. As to be expected, a few years ago it did require an extensive make-over but the service was not interrupted whilst rebuilding work was carried out. Temporary accommodation was found for the unit in another part of the hospital which incidentally, amalgamated with Guys in 1993 becoming Guy's and St. Thomas' Hospital NHS Trust.

Battling on at The Copse

It was a bitter blow to us all when closure of the Larkshall Unit was announced. It had given us peace of mind to know that if Peter had a staffing problem, they would always find a bed for him there, with nursing staff who knew how to care for him, until he was able to return to his own home. Joan Corry would be taking early retirement and the rest of her team would be split up going to different establishments to work, some in the NHS but others finding jobs in the private sector. In spite of all the local protests we were told it was no longer viable to keep this small unit open. Only a very small part of Chingford Hospital but including the therapy department would remain open. The rest of the place would be demolished and the site sold for housing. Peter would still be able to visit for physiotherapy each week, as his admirable therapist Mara was continuing in her post but that was all.

How would we manage his care package and who could act as line manager for the girls? After many deliberations and meetings with the finance officer of the local Health Authority, it was decided the best solution would be to make me totally responsible for Peter's package. For some time, Peter and I had become more and more involved in the advertising, interviewing and selecting of his staff but always under the auspices of the Larkshall Unit. To actually manage the girls completely, balance the books and keep detailed accounts, required more expertise and I didn't know if I had the necessary skills required for this. It meant I would have complete control of his budget, which was set and reviewed annually. This included an amount for other expenses, such as replacement of certain necessary pieces of medical equipment and overheads, apart from the money required for salaries, national insurance, advertising costs etc. We knew how to organise weekly rotas and annual leave etc., and I suppose if I got into real trouble, I could always say so and ask for a care manager to be appointed. For now, Peter was keen for us to try and manage the whole thing ourselves and as usual, he was right. In some ways it was easier for the girls – at least they saw their employer on a daily basis.

I learned as I went along, having no previous experience in pay roll, human resources or accountancy. Still I did have one big advantage. Dave had now retired from work and his help was invaluable. I involved Peter in all decisions and I know he enjoyed being consulted when there were choices to be made.

Things gradually settled down at The Copse and we scraped by without too many problems of a financial nature. The girls had always come to me if they had a grievance which was more often than not about the rota and who was working when. I tried to prepare this for three months at a time but of course it was always subject to change for various reasons. Peter was normally the first to hear when a carer wasn't happy and more often than not, he told me how he wanted the matter resolved. He could be very kind and understanding most of the time but also quite inflexible if he thought someone was taking advantage of him. He was always quick to make amends, however, if he had made a mistake or lost his temper (yes he could argue with his carers or me) and tell us to get lost in no uncertain terms. When he had calmed down there was always a bunch of flowers or card to say sorry. It must have been so frustrating for him to have a heated disagreement with someone but at the same time having to rely on that very person to spell out his point of view. His normal way of dealing with this situation was to ask to be pushed into his garden or if very cold, into a room on his own, given a glass of alcohol and left alone for a while.

His personality came through in spite of everything. As a small boy he had a temper but an outburst never lasted for long and he was always prepared to say he was sorry. Once an argument was over, it was forgotten and there were no recriminations. He had the happy knack of being able to channel his thoughts in other directions and I am sure his garden played a part in this. He had paid to have this mainly paved so it was suitable for his wheelchair and he could keep an eye on his precious shrubs. He spent a good deal of time out there issuing instructions as to what needed weeding or watering.

Peter planned his week's activities himself, taking into consideration the likes and dislikes of the carer who happened to be working each day. Linda was particularly keen on gardening and a trip was often arranged to a garden centre where they would spend an afternoon wandering round the greenhouses, maybe buying a few bedding plants or yet another shrub. They liked to fit in a halt for refreshments if there was a suitable venue nearby. He loved the forest and countryside and would visit the places accessible for wheelchair users whenever he could.

Another favourite outing was to Southend on Sea, the nearest coastal town. We would often accompany him or alternatively meet him there. We always started at the Cliffs Pavilion where even if the weather was inclement, he could be warm and cosy. Here, he was protected from the elements and yet still able to appreciate a good view of the sea. The Thames barges on the estuary were quite visible from the very large windows of the building. I would prepare a picnic, Peter would buy the drinks at the bar in the Pavilion and we could while away a few pleasant hours. If it wasn't too cold, he liked to go along the seafront and maybe for a ride on the train which plies back and forth along the pier, or a meal at one of the seafront restaurants. He always enjoyed the day whatever the weather and wherever we went.

He was not so fond of the winter months because he felt the cold dreadfully and his activities were therefore, somewhat restricted during this season. He spent more time in the warmth of his own home and so was particularly pleased when friends and relatives dropped by always seeing he had refreshments to offer them. He himself was particularly keen on a lemon drizzle cake that Margaret, our sister in law, used to make for him.

A trip to the local multi screen cinema was often arranged especially if he thought a particular carer would enjoy the film being shown or he would treat one or two of his small relatives to an appropriate screening. He was always eager to please the children, with trips to a Zoo, Nature Park or even just a burger bar if this is what they fancied. Children were a very important part of his life and he valued their friendship.

Sundays he usually came to a family dinner at our house and most of the girls were pleased to accompany him to this I think. At least they didn't have to do the cooking on that day! Normally his visit was preceded by a trip to the public library for a supply of videos etc. for viewing the following week. The rest of our family were good to Peter and he usually had at least one invitation per week to a meal either at his brother, sister Julie's house or alternatively to a cousin and their respective family. I know he particularly enjoyed these visits where there were young children involved. He might never have children of his own but it didn't stop him sharing in his relatives or indeed his carers' offspring. He would spend an enormous amount of time choosing appropriate gifts for each of the children he knew when their own birthday came around. His Christmas list was endless but this was one way he could pay back some of the hospitality and kindness shown to him by so many people. His own birthday was usually celebrated at the nearby public house which had an activity area where all the youngsters would go when they had tired of adult conversation. The proprietors allowed us to re-arrange the furniture so we could all be together for a meal and we would celebrate his day with a cake and noisy rendition of happy birthday.

He never lost his love of Christmas and involved himself in everything connected with the festive season. This normally started Christmas Eve afternoon when we all went to our local church for the Crib service. Peter and his carer were given places right at the front so he didn't miss any of the nativity play usually performed by children. Then later, after he had inspected our house to approve the long table laid for the next day's special meal for around thirty relatives, we would be ready to travel to the traditional Christmas Eve party at one of the other relative's houses. If Peter did have a carer working during the day on the 25th, then she would bring him over ready to eat with us all. Otherwise, Dave would go to The Copse and bring Peter back where we could look after him for the rest of the day. Persuading carers to work over holiday periods can be a bit difficult and if a girl wanted to be with her own family during the day time at Christmas we could accommodate her wishes. We didn't really mind at all as there were so many willing hands to tend Peter's needs. Even the very young ones liked to help and I know sometimes he could have almost a day's eye drops used in the space of a just one single hour. The little ones needed a step ladder or something similar to reach him but they wanted to do their bit and using the eye dropper was one thing within their capabilities. He never complained and I'm sure he secretly enjoyed all the attention even if sometimes their efforts were a little over zealous. I was preoccupied with food for the crowd and more often than not, it was cousins-in-law Sue or Helen who fed Peter with his Christmas fare.

One Christmas when we only had limited cover, Dave was taking him back alone to his own home where he would be meeting the overnight carer at a specified time. This was a normal procedure for the time of year and she would then take over and arrange Peter's bedtime routine. However no sooner had they left our house and entered the main High Street in Loughton, when a disaster occurred. Peter had been lifted back in his wheelchair before they set off to make him more comfortable but unfortunately, the belt which held him in position had not been refastened again after his lift. Suddenly, he slid forward coming completely out of his chair, landing squashed in the well of the car on his back, leaving no room for manoeuvre. Catastrophe! What could they do? There was no way Dave could rectify the situation on his own but they couldn't make the rest of the journey like this. They couldn't alert us to their predicament or Peter's carer who would be waiting for him at The Copse. They didn't have a mobile telephone with them and unfortunately, nobody seemed to be around who they could approach for help. Motorists are a bit wary about being flagged down around midnight and the windows of Peter's car were tinted so it wasn't obvious there was a wheelchair passenger inside in dire need of assistance. He was getting cold and finding breathing difficult due to his awkward position. Finally a young man did stop his car and after a great effort, they got Peter back in his chair but it taught us all a lesson. Always make sure the belt is securely fastened before setting off on a car journey.

Peter did like to feel useful and spent much time pondering what he could do to help. When I was ever away with my Brownie Pack, I could always rely on him to write a letter for a child who didn't normally receive one from home and he made sure his dad was looked after until I came back, asking him round to dinner for a change. Occasionally he could act as a tester for a brownie or scout badge. I know Paul and Sue's son James did his cook's badge under Peter's direction at The Copse and then they all ate the quite professional dinner he produced. He always had a competition with his nephew, Oliver, about who could grow the tallest sunflower in their own garden. Oliver was in charge of the measuring with one of Peter's carers acting as judge.

He made it his business to try and cheer someone up if they were going through a difficult patch or they were feeling a bit low. I recall when his cousin Debbie first confided to him that she was pregnant for the third time, and feeling apprehensive about the age gap there would be between their two teenage girls and the expected new arrival. Peter was quick to reassure her. The very next day he arrived at her house with a huge basket crammed with all the paraphernalia she would need for a new baby. Her apprehension turned to excitement as she examined each item in the basket and remembered how she had enjoyed the baby days of her other two girls. Now she would look forward to the new birth.

Chest infections were an ever present worry because his breathing could deteriorate rapidly if the early signs of a problem were not nipped in the bud. Dr. Drake was a most understanding general practitioner and he allowed Peter to always have a spare course of antibiotics so he could start treatment immediately there were any signs or symptoms of trouble brewing. Even so, every couple of years an infection would fail to respond to this first line of treatment and a spell in hospital was required to aid his recovery.

I suppose really he kept remarkably healthy all things considered and I am sure this had a lot to do with the care and attention given to him by his team of carers.

Peter in his garden

James 'the cook'

Playing dominos with nephew Henry

Oliver measuring Peter's Sunflower

Carers

It was essential for Peter's well being to have a good team of carers who enjoyed their work with him and who were one hundred per cent loyal, conscientious and reliable. They also had to get on with each other being prepared to adopt a flexible approach with their shifts if the need arose. In addition, although they did not normally work together, a hand over each morning was required when they could report on the previous day's happenings. It was unrealistic to expect saints to apply for the job and in any case, I don't think it would have suited Peter at all to have paragons of virtue engaged! He would have found it far too boring.

Of course we made many mistakes initially and it took a number of years before we felt confident we were adopting the right approach to engaging and keeping staff. One particular time I recall we were really worried about the recruitment of a new carer. In spite of advertisements in the local press, we hadn't managed to find anyone suitable. Each advertisement placed cost money but in addition, too frequently placed ads in the situations vacant column of the same paper could also create a bad impression on suitable job seekers. I felt very worried about finding a new carer to complete the team and Dave had sent me off for a bit of retail therapy whilst he manned the telephone in case of any enquirers. I left him with a paper giving full details of all the things the job entailed and questions to ask any possible caller. When I returned, he was quite excited. He said he had just spoken to a young lady from Peru, who could speak excellent English. Whilst Peter didn't have any objections to employing people from other countries, a good command of the English language was essential if they were going to be able to communicate with him. This young lady answered positively to all the questions Dave asked and was eager to meet Peter. An interview was arranged and eventually Millie was employed. This was the start of a long association with carers from South America – ironic really when you remember Peter was saving to visit this part of the world when he had his accident.

Ideally, his team consisted of a mix of five full and part-time carers. This made best use of his funding as there were not so many overheads with part-time staff. It also allowed us to utilise the services of foreign nationals who were in this country mainly to improve their English, but who were permitted to work a few hours each week to supplement their grants. Weekend shifts suited them best as their lessons were normally on a Monday to Friday basis. They had often been involved in care in the community on a voluntary basis before coming to

England and providing their language skills were reasonable, they fitted in well.

Before Millie had to move on, she had introduced us to Rocio, a friend from her schooldays in Peru. It seems as though Peter was always having changes in his staff but this was partly as a result of employing females. For one thing, young ladies have a tendency to get pregnant and maternity leave creates a temporary gap in the team. Rocio had endless patience and helped him no end with his computer programmes. Between the two of them, they designed and printed many Christmas and birthday cards for family and friends each year. She was still working part time for Peter when he died, even though she had married and taken maternity leave three times over the years. This produced three more little girls to learn to love and tend Peter's needs plus another one born to Millie.

Peter described having carers as being married to five different women, each with their own characteristics and special qualities. He valued every one of them and the variety their diverse personalities brought to the job made his life more interesting. He said they kept him busy trying to accommodate their different tastes in food, music, television and other forms of entertainment.

There were several more South American girls who worked for Peter over the years but I know at this stage, he would want me to mention Idaly who came from Colombia. For a time they were quite close and she introduced him to many of her friends from her homeland inviting him to parties and social events. She never lost touch and always had a special bond with him, even after she met and married another Englishman.

There were three English girls who worked for Peter for longer than any others – namely Karen, Sharon and later Linda. They were all very different but highly valued members of his team whilst they were with him. Karen of course stayed with him for more years than anyone else and although she was not all sweetness and light, she had the right attitude towards disabled people. I know she cared deeply for Peter and his well-being and wanted him included in so many things. She was always enthusiastic about her various hobbies and had him made an honorary member of the club where she played bowls, introducing him to other members who all made him feel so welcome when he visited. Sharon had an excellent sense of humour, was very chatty and always had some good stories to relate to Peter when she came to work. He really missed her when she decided she must start a degree course in nursing and therefore leave Peter's employ. Linda was already a trained carer when she came to him as a replacement for Sharon. She was a very practical and capable girl, extremely strong and like Peter, loved the forest and countryside.

Karin, who came from Bloemfontein, South Africa, also deserves a mention here. She was very young but so mature and capable for her age. She didn't have any real experience of care work when we first met her but she learned so fast and became an excellent carer when she was with Peter for the last year of his life.

These carers became part of our family once they came to work for Peter. Our relatives and friends accepted them as such and they were included in all our family gatherings and outings, being invited to meals and parties at their various homes.

Karen

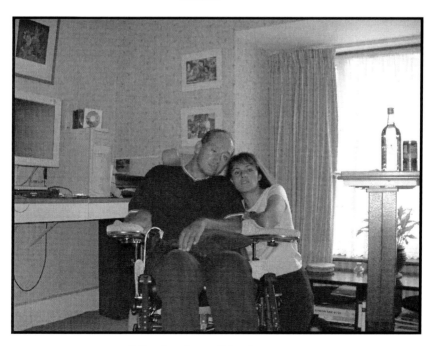

Monica from Mexico

Sharon and Rocio on holiday in Tenerife

Karin and Peter in his garden

Linda

Mireya with Peter

Rocio

Millie

Peter with Idaly

Karen's wedding

Sharon's wedding

Holidays and Excursions

In spite of his disabilities, Peter never lost his lust for travel although trips did take rather more careful planning after his accident and he did have to be selective about suitable places to visit. Holidays in the sun particularly appealed to him, especially when we were in the depths of a typical cold damp English winter.

His favourite place was Port Richey on the gulf side of Florida where he always hired a very attractive wheelchair friendly villa for a couple of weeks at a time. It was owned by an Englishman with spinal injuries himself so it had been adapted to a very high standard with wide doors, no steps to negotiate and plenty of turning space for a wheelchair. In addition, the swimming pool was extra warm and came complete with a hoist so Peter could use it. The location of the villa was spacious and serene with a large lake at the bottom of the garden and an accessible fishing dock where Peter liked to sit and watch the wild life about their business. In the middle was an island where the egrets used to roost in the trees at night and the lake itself had an abundance of fish, small turtles and its own resident alligator which could be a bit scary when it decided to climb the bank and do a spot of sunbathing.

Florida is ideal for people in wheelchairs because it is very flat and has a good climate, which is why so many Vietnam veterans choose to live there. Everyone treated Peter well and even the children didn't stare as if he was some oddity who had escaped from a freak show. All places of interest were accessible for wheelchair patrons and usually entrance fees were waived or reduced for them or their carers.

Another big attraction for Peter was the fact that his dad's brother Eric would fly in from his home in Virginia to stay at the villa whilst we were there. Of course before he had his accident, Peter and Eldita stayed with Eric in Virginia when they first arrived in the United States many moons ago. It must have been difficult for Eric the first time he joined us in Florida. Of course he knew all about the results of the accident from us over the ensuing years, but nothing could quite prepare him from seeing the dramatic change in the young fit, athletic Peter he remembered. Also it was less than a year since Bertha, his own dear wife had died. She had been very disabled and housebound herself as a result of rheumatoid arthritis and Eric had been her only carer. Nonetheless, he kept his feelings in check and was a great asset in helping with Peter's care. He was so strong, he could lift Peter almost unaided and he was happy to push him anywhere which gave the girls a break. He thought they were doing a wonderful job and was only too pleased to help them in any way possible.

One funny incident occurred on this first visit of Eric though. He had been having very restless nights following his wife's death and wouldn't just talk in his sleep – he ranted and raved, waking anyone within earshot. I was worried that if Peter's girls had their slumbers disturbed, they would be miserable and unable to carry out their tasks the next day. We only normally took two carers with us whereas at home there would be at least three sharing the work each week. Dave explained the situation to Eric who was oblivious to his night time activities and most upset to think he was disturbing the rest of us. He decided it would be best if he slept in the large garage at the front of the house where there was already a spare bed. Here he would be out of earshot of the occupants of the bedrooms and he assured us he would be quite comfy there. All he needed was a bucket to act as a chamber pot in case it was necessary to relieve himself during the night after consuming a considerable number of beers as was his long time habit. All went well until about three am when he needed his brother's assistance. Apparently he had got up to use his temporary pee pot and by mistake, instead of turning the light on, he had activated the switch for the garage door which had rolled completely open. He was now exposed to the elements and needed the remote key to close the door unless he was prepared to sleep in full view of anyone passing the house until we were up and about the next morning. Of course we were now all awake and laughing our heads off at the situation when suddenly Peter's buzzer echoed through the house bringing our merriment to an abrupt halt. He didn't intend to be left out of things and wanted to know exactly what was so funny in the middle of the night.

The biggest drawback to holidays in Florida for Peter was always the length of the flight. He didn't really want to waste any of his own money or the respite grant he received from social services towards his holiday, on upgraded seats so always travelled economy class. British Airways were very good to him and Lord Marshall's personal assistant used to oversee our booking and make sure he got bulkhead seats with extra leg room. In fact, the first time we travelled to Florida with B.A. she arranged a bottle of champagne for Peter, to get his holiday off to a good start. All his medical paraphernalia would be packed in two large blue crates (like removal companies use) and labelled with a Red Cross and list of contents. This way we didn't have to pay excess baggage charges and his boxes were never damaged or went astray. Peter's wheelchair was also given special treatment. He stayed in it right till he got to the door of the aircraft. Then it was all hands to the deck. All removable bits of the wheelchair such as the arms, legs, headrest etc. were taken inside the aircraft and stored in the overhead lockers, before the frame went into the hold. One of us would slide his special Roho cushion out from under his buttocks and have this ready for him to sit on when he was carried to his seat on the plane. We always got on the aircraft first and so were able to make sure he was comfortably installed in his seat before the rest of the passengers came on board. We did as much preparation work as possible before Peter took to the air and always reminded the airline of his special needs. Of course, sometimes there were hitches but nothing we couldn't cope with.

The other consideration when planning holidays was transport once we arrived at our destination. In the United States of America, this was comparatively easy although quite an expensive add-on. We needed a van large enough to hold two carers, Dave, me and Peter in his wheelchair, because transferring him to a seat was not really an option. A company called 'Wheelchair Getaways' has accessible vans for rental and these could be made available at the arrival airport. The driving was normally always done solely by Dave as none of Peter's carers felt happy about being in charge of such a large vehicle and on the wrong side of the road at that!

We didn't travel around very much once we arrived at the villa. It took Peter a couple of days to recoup from the flight and then there were good beaches within a few miles so long journeys were unnecessary. We would just do two or three special outings during our time at the villa – maybe to St. Petersburg or Tarpon Springs where he could be accommodated on a boat trip to see dolphins etc., followed by a special meal courtesy of Eric, at one of the many Greek restaurants overlooking the river. I think his all time favourite was a trip to Homosassa Springs where he could take another boat trip down the river and get very close to the Manatees they had in the wild life refuge there.

Over the years Peter also went to other holiday resorts nearer to home. He liked the Algarve in Portugal, where once again, it was possible to rent a suitable villa and the necessary transport, courtesy of a company owned by another disabled man. The advantage here was that Julie and Fergie plus boys would also stay in adjoining premises so it was much more a family holiday and of course less costly. Peter did like to have the children around him and they loved the private swimming pool that came with the villa which was set a few miles from the coast, in the mountain region with beautiful views all around. We did not venture far when we stayed at this resort either. There really wasn't any need; we would buy our provisions at the nearest supermarket about five miles away, supplemented by the fresh fruit etc. which we were allowed to pick ourselves and generally ate at the villa. Lunch would be an al fresco buffet meal around the pool and dinner was often a barbeque, again eaten outside but at the table this time, washed down with a few glasses of wine and surrounded by the bougainvillea and sweet smelling jasmine which abounded around our holiday home. We all used to like to go to the pool area at the end of the day and watch the sun setting over the mountains – a truly magnificent sight.

On one occasion, we took the whole family plus two of Peter's carers, for a holiday on the island of Cyprus. We stayed in a place called Latchi village where we booked four apartments; one for each family plus a specially adapted apartment for Peter and his girls. We managed to get disabled transport to ferry Peter back and forth to the airport but apart from this, we just stayed within the village complex itself. There was plenty going on here during the day to suit the tastes of all members of our party and Peter was spoilt for choice as a spectator. Of course the swimming pools were a big attraction but another favourite was a different type of pool played with the aid of snooker cues. The young ones loved this and I know it brought back memories to Peter of when he used to think himself somewhat of a champion at his local club. I recall when he was only a lad, he took my father to his club after boasting of his skill with a cue and beat him at the game.

The beach was only a short walk away and there were enough restaurants on the waterfront for us to sample a different one each evening. It was late in the season when we visited Latchi so it wasn't very busy. However, the weather was perfect and as a party of fourteen, any restaurant was more than happy to welcome us to their establishment. The only snag with Latchi village was the steep slopes to negotiate around the complex which are somewhat tiring when pushing a heavy wheelchair. I marvel at how Rocio managed on this holiday because she was already expecting her second baby and must have felt exhausted at times. She did not even tell any of us about her pregnancy until after we had returned home because she was determined to pull her weight with the chores and didn't want any concessions made because of her condition. Thank goodness we had David and Fergie to take care of pushing Peter's wheelchair for the majority of the time.

English holidays Peter enjoyed after his accident, often took place at Blagdon Farm in Devon. Here there were eight fully accessible cottages set in more than ten acres of peaceful Devonshire countryside about fifteen miles from Bude. All of the bungalows overlooked a very large fishing lake with views of forests and fields in the distance. I remember Fergie and carer Linda fishing on this lake and us all having a beautiful trout supper on one occasion. The farm had its own specially built indoor heated swimming and hydrotherapy pool, a games barn, outdoor playground and a small animal enclosure so of course this was another venue very popular with the rest of the family especially the children. We didn't have to cope with the difficulties of air travel when visiting

Blagdon Farm but Peter did find the car journey a bit exhausting even though we had several stops en route.

Peter also managed to visit other holiday places in spite of his disabilities included Tenerife and mainland Spain. Thanks are due to Social Services for the respite grants they gave him once a year towards his forthcoming planned holiday which always meant so much to him.

Apart from holidays, Peter was also fond of day trips to locations that were just a little bit different to his usual routine. I know he particularly enjoyed a visit to the Chelsea Flower Show when he was given special tickets enabling him and ourselves to attend before the show actually opened **even** to members.

We did feel slightly embarrassed by one trip organised for him to visit the top of Canary Wharf. We had a friend who worked for the director of the building and she had gone to a great deal of trouble to arrange special passes so Peter could visit on a Sunday when no other members of the public were allowed entry. Unfortunately, Peter had become rather acrophobic since having his accident and he couldn't be persuaded to go anywhere near the windows to look down on the magnificent scene spread out below. Anyway, we enjoyed the day and Peter liked the photos we were able to show him later.

His cousin Stephen sometimes accompanied him on a day trip to France. They would travel in Peter's car after having removed the little side seats in the back to make more room for goodies from the duty free stores they always visited before returning home. I think by the time Peter had asked everyone else what they would like, there wasn't a lot of time or room for many purchases for his own consumption.

Just to mention one more memorable outing he had with an old friend of his. Martin arranged to take Peter and his father to a film set to see Pierce Bronson who was working on the James Bond film 'Golden Eye'. After watching the day's shooting, they were introduced to the star himself who chatted with Peter and gave him a signed photograph as a memento of the day.

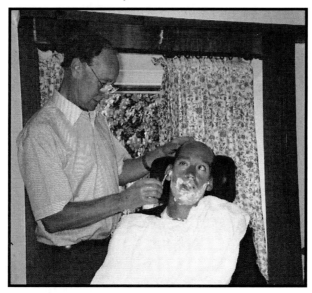

Giving the girls a break in Portugal

On the Fishing Dock at Port Richey, Florida.

Meet up with Eric in Florida

Edward and Peter at Blagdon Farm.

At the Chelsea Flower Show.

Peter's Writings

The most important work that Peter did was to compose his care handbook. Eventually it became a very sophisticated instruction and guidance manual for every new carer who came to work for him. However, in the first place it was just a simple care plan for each day. The difficulties involved in getting the huge funding needed for twenty four hour care were almost insurmountable especially in the days before equal opportunities etc. The Independent Living Fund had just been set up though and we were told if we could justify our request for help from them, there was a good chance they would agree to part-fund Peter. First though, it would be necessary to explain what care was needed for him each hour of the day and night. This was the beginning of the care book. Like Topsy, it just grew. Of course it always included a page on his special communication system, which was about the only thing that didn't change over the years. I have not included the manual within this book; suffice to say it included chapters on all aspects of his care, tips on carrying out necessary tasks, his interests, likes and dislikes, all written with a sense of humour and the quick wit so typical of Peter. On a lighter note, Peter loved his computer and did compose a number of poems on various subjects, - a few of which are printed below:

Monica   (A carer)

Monica comes from
'Down Mexico way'
Alan looks after the baby
So she can work in the day

She has a degree in philology
A strange qualification
For working with me
Has a good figure
But is always watching her weight
I think you are what you are
And that is fate.

Alan is her husband
He was Manchester born
They met when in Israel
On a kibbutz - picking corn.

They have another child
Lauren is her name
She is just eight years of age
Being bi-lingual is her claim to fame.
They all live in a gaily painted flat
All are very happy
And that is that

My Cat

> I don't like my cat
> It's as simple as that
> I wish she was warmer
> I preferred my former
> He would sit on my lap all day
> Why did a car have to take him away?

(This cat, called Florence could not control her claws and Peter would often suffer scratches as a result – the one who was run over, called Leonard was Peter's all time favourite)

Window

All winter through the window I stare
In the warmth of my kitchen, the garden I prepare
It will soon be summer and I can go out again
With the help of my carers, I will try to explain
How I want my garden to be
For its appearance means a lot to me.

Peters Garden

D Day

Tomorrow is bowel day
I hate it!
Such a performance
Just to have a Tom-tit.

I have to lie in my bed
To have a dump
It's very awkward
It gives me the hump!

I wish I was normal
And could sit on the throne
But my legs don't work –
Still I shouldn't moan.

Even though it takes over an hour
At least I can get up after
And have a shower.

Idaly

Idaly is short but very compact
Can just see over my head
That's not a lie – it is a fact
She works a lot – not only for me
Has a job in the city
At a club – the R.A.C.

Has a house in London
She lives all alone
She rents out her rooms
To help pay for her home

I would like to look after dear Idaly
But she needs a real man
Not broken like me!

Her sister is visiting
She's here with her boy
He keeps them awake at night
Playing with his toys

At Christmas
She's visiting her family and mother
It's a long way to go though
They live in Columbia!

Apart from his poetry, Peter always designed and printed his own stationery. He took enormous pleasure from designing his greetings and one can only marvel at the patience he showed when working on a project. The outside cover of his Christmas greeting cards often included a cameo of each girl working for him during that particular year and birthday cards were always appropriate for the recipient and something to be treasured for a long time. I know everyone felt honoured to receive one of Peter's cards.

He had managed to enrol on a computer course with Southampton University who specialised in distance learning for people with special needs. Each month they would send him a disc with work to be done. On completion, he returned his work for marking. The girls also benefited from this and several of them learned their computer skills just by sitting with Peter in front of the computer screen.

The course also helped him to obtain a grant towards a new computer with a larger screen which was easier on his eyes. I could always tell when I called to see him if he had been working for too long. His eyes were so inflamed, bright red and sore looking. He found it frustrating that he could only work for a comparatively short time, especially when the task in hand was so fascinating to him. The indent in his eyebrow made by the wheel on the special spectacles he wore to operate the computer would be so pronounced, there was no denying he had been working for too long and his eyes were badly in need of a rest. The worst scenario though was when he actually had an infection in his eyes because the medication required to clear this up, blurred his vision even more than usual and he couldn't see to operate his beloved computer or even watch television. Then, all he could do would be to plan things in his head for action when his sight improved once more.

Wired for thought

By the year 1994, sophisticated electronics and micro technology were making great strides in the field of medical science and implants in the brain were no longer confined to the realms of science fiction. Every so often our attention would be drawn to articles in the press and we wondered how long it would be before maybe something was invented that could help Peter. He himself was down to earth and quite philosophical about the various newspaper cuttings we showed him; he never expected miracles but gave me permission to do some research on his behalf to see if there was the smallest chance of any invention being appropriate to his needs.

He realised he couldn't have a new brain stem but queried the possibility of an implant to give him an automatic blink. This would hopefully completely cure his 'dry eye' syndrome and mean he could spend longer pursuing his favourite occupation working with his computer. The gold weight inserted in his eyelid at Moorfields Hospital protected his eye from further damage but couldn't do anything to alleviate the dryness and lack of lubrication to the eye. I wrote to several professors in the field of biomedical engineering based in this country and abroad, also including Dr. Frankel at Stoke Mandeville to see if anyone could offer any suggestions. We were beginning to despair of getting any positive responses when we had a letter from Mr. Teddy who had carried out the original surgery to fit Peter's pacemaker system. Dr. Frankel had acquainted him with our pleas and he said he knew an emeritus professor in neuro-prosthetics who might be interested in helping him. We couldn't wait to meet this great man.

Our first appointment with Professor Giles Brindley was at the Royal National Orthopaedic Hospital, Stanmore, on the 5th December 1994. He was a quiet, unassuming man who listened very carefully to the potted history we gave him, followed by Peter's hopes and aspirations for the future. After some thought, he said he had several ideas but wanted to come and see Peter in his own environment before elaborating further on what he might be able to achieve. This was the start of a long association with Professor Brindley and the beginning of a new chapter in Peter's life.

It wasn't too long before Professor Brindley, true to his word, came to see Peter at The Copse to talk to us about his proposals. As he reiterated, because Peter's brain stem was damaged beyond repair, no electrical signals sent by his brain could pass through here and reach their appropriate destination. He was suggesting using a battery of electrodes over the area of Peter's brain that controlled movements and could pick up the signals being transmitted. These signals could then bypass the brain stem, be amplified and changed via a transmitter so they could be recognised and used through a computer. It sounded like rocket science to us but the idea in its simplest form was that by thinking 'left' or 'right' Peter would be able to move a cursor on his computer screen. This simple action would ultimately result in him being far less reliant on other people. He could become more in command himself and take responsibility for his own decisions without outside interference.

We were most concerned about any interference with Peter's brain and wanted assurance that the proposed implants were not going to make things worse for him. At the moment, at least he had his full senses and could lead a so called 'independent' lifestyle, even though this was extremely restricted by his severe disabilities. The one thing he could do, albeit very slowly, was communicate with other people but what if an implant caused him to lose the ability to raise his one precious eyebrow? How would he be able to converse in this scenario? Peter adopted a more cavalier attitude and was all for pressing ahead, although even he grudgingly admitted it would be a retrograde step to interfere with his only useful movement of the one eyebrow. One of the proposals, which I believe entailed placing an electrode actually inside his brain, did carry a risk of epilepsy as a side effect. His father and I were adamant he should not take the risk and for once Peter didn't disagree with us so this option was shelved.

Eventually it was decided that Professor Brindley would work on the idea of a telemetry system which avoided placing anything actually inside Peter's brain, at least for the time being. Electrodes would be placed on the outer surface of the brain with wires trailing down to several other electronic components culminating in a receiver in his thigh muscle. Of course, much research was necessary and many experiments had to be carried out before an operation could actually become feasible. This research and eventual surgery could not be funded by the National Health Service but once again, Sir Jimmy Savile came to the rescue, promising he would sort out the financial side of things and see that the money was available for the project to go forward; we were not to worry about this aspect.

For the next eighteen months, Professor Brindley became a regular visitor to The Copse. He would arrive with a battery of equipment, all very rudimentary, and would immediately get to work with Peter. Often he had already tried prototypes on himself in his workshop before he came. We understood that this was how he had worked in the past with previous inventions to assist people with disabilities. He was incredibly patient and never appeared frustrated when things didn't go according to plan. Just the journey alone through the busy traffic right across London could not have been easy for him but I remember on at least one occasion he arrived only to find he was missing a vital piece of equipment which meant he had had a wasted journey and it was necessary for him to come back the following day. At first, the electrodes and wires were just taped to Peter's skin all the way from his head to half way down his leg. It was difficult to visualise how there would be room for all this to fit into Peter's body when the operation was actually carried out, without causing severe rejection problems. However, slowly Prof. Brindley made progress; gradually, the proposed implants looked slightly more sophisticated and by the spring of 1996 he announced he was ready to plan for the surgery to take place.

The operation would be carried out by Mr. Peter J. Teddy at The Radcliffe Infirmary at Oxford. Surgery was scheduled for the 18th July 1996 but before this Mr. Teddy and his anaesthetist, Dr. Westbrook wanted to visit Peter at The Copse. Mr. Teddy explained to us that the device they were proposing to insert was a world first and had huge potential for helping other people with similar problems. For this reason, the BBC was interested in filming the procedure and making a documentary programme about Peter and the operation being performed. He wanted Peter's permission for the BBC to become involved and explained the potential to raise funds for future research would be greatly enhanced by such a programme. Peter was delighted and couldn't wait to meet the T.V. crew.

I suppose we all learned a lot about making television programmes over the ensuing few months and I know Peter found it fun, thoroughly enjoying this chapter of his life. I think at first his neighbours wondered what on earth was going on when they witnessed all the activity, the comings and goings of the technicians, cameraman and reporter etc. What did the very large arc lights used to illuminate his garden, where some of the filming took place, mean? Had their flatmate discovered hidden treasure or something? We had a lot of explaining to do to put their minds at ease. As for the T.V. people, they seemed to spend a great deal of their time outside Peter's front door where they could obtain the best reception for their mobile cell phones. Mobiles were not yet commonplace in the community and suitable antenna masts were few and far between. Peter wanted all his 'guests' taken care of and liked to see they were amply supplied with food and drink whilst they were at The Copse. The girls who were working for Peter at that time took care of this and seemed to enjoy the distraction from their usual more mundane tasks.

The reporter was a lovely compassionate and thoughtful young lady by the name of Shahnaz Pakravan. She quickly developed a rapport with Peter, discussing many aspects of his life and even trying to sort out suitable holiday destinations she thought would appeal to him. She was most professional in the way she approached her work and later was even present in the operating theatre whilst the surgery was taking place, although I am sure she didn't find this an easy part of her job. The plan was to make a documentary suitable for screening on 'Tomorrow's World' being transmitted on BBC1 in early autumn. It would include a short introduction of Peter and his present situation, the surgery itself, after care and early results. Some time later in the year there would be a follow up programme, hopefully showing how progress had changed Peter's life.

Just filming the first part took several visits to The Copse, Professor Brindley's workshop and the department of Neurosurgery at The Radcliffe Infirmary. On the day of Peter's admission to the hospital, a camera crew arrived very early at The Copse intent on following Peter so as not to miss out a single detail of his eventful journey to Oxford. A telephone link was established between Peter's car and the TV vehicle so nothing important would be missed. I think Dave felt more than a little apprehensive about being given instructions to aid their photography on the extremely busy M40 Motorway, especially when the BBC car pulled up alongside and a head and shoulders appeared out of the sliding window complete with camera. Incidentally, none of these shots were actually used in the final documentary.

Peter was admitted two days before the actual operation took place so that all the necessary preliminaries could be carried out including brain scans to define the exact position of the motor cortex over which the main implant would be fixed. There would be twenty electrodes in this main component and then wires would be fed down from here, through his body linking to boosters and finally finishing up in a transmitter located in his thigh. It all sounded like science fiction to us mere mortals and we were petrified but Peter, true to form appeared quite relaxed about the whole affair.

The operation took nearly six hours but once it was all over and he had been moved to the intensive care department, we were able to see him again. It had been a very long and tense day for us all. Professor Brindley had come out from theatre as soon as the actual surgery was complete to let us know it had gone well and that Peter was being moved to the recovery bay but now we could see him. His head was swathed in bandages, he was on a ventilator and there were tubes and monitors all over him but we felt reassured as soon as we spoke to him. The eyebrow was working perfectly and he could communicate with us. Who cared that the TV cameras were filming our every reaction at this critical time?

Peter spent the rest of the day in the intensive care department before he was moved to his own room to recuperate. His brother called to visit him just three days after surgery and we couldn't believe it when he reported to us on Peter's progress. He said he was up in his wheelchair and they had both visited the pub opposite the hospital for a celebratory pint! For once, the TV cameras weren't present to record this stage of his recovery. Peter was an amazingly resilient and determined character.

The first testing of the implants took place six days after surgery. Peter's small room at the hospital was bursting at the seams what with the medical staff, family and of course the TV crew all crammed into such a small space. It was a wonder Professor Brindley could find room for his apparatus. Also electrical signals from the bed and other nursing paraphernalia were interfering with the professor's equipment and eventually the experiment was deferred until Peter was able to return home where trials could take place in a quieter and more peaceful atmosphere.

Subsequently it transpired that the last component in the set-up, (the encoder which converts the brain signal into a recognisable computer signal) was faulty and Peter had to have a second operation to replace this before testing could begin in earnest. Sadly, in spite of months of experiments, adjustments and retests the system did not work for Peter and in actual fact, he had to have one of the implants removed a few years later as it was creating skin problems. In spite of all this, Peter never regretted having taken part in the experiments; he said he wasn't at all surprised it didn't work for him because he was the first 'guinea pig' but he hoped it would be useful for other people in the future.

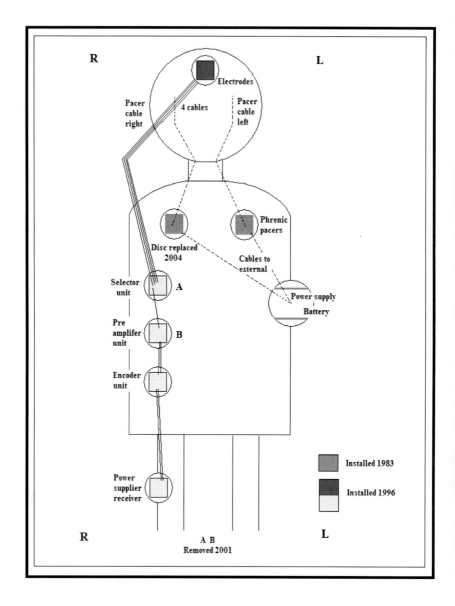

Peter – the Bionic man. Chart showing all his implants.

Last few years at The Copse

In September 2001, Peter took delivery of his new car, the bright red Ford Galaxy which had apparently belonged to Princess Margaret for a short time after she had a stroke. This was his last and most luxurious car and it became his pride and joy. From the outside, it didn't look like transport for a disabled person and he loved the compact disc player and other little luxuries which were fitted before he took delivery. It was very spacious inside and even more comfortable than the Nissan which had served him well for over twelve years. I don't know how someone could stoop to stealing the hub caps from this, his brand new car whilst it was parked in the disabled bay outside his own flat but this is what one misguided wretch did one night after Peter had gone to bed. I think even he was a bit upset for a while. Then he said the hub caps must be replaced quickly or the crook might come back for the wheels next time. However, he would just like a cheap set of alloy caps which would be less of a temptation to a potential robber. Maybe the thief was the same person who stole his hanging baskets soon after they were planted and hung outside his front door earlier in the year!

His other big acquisition was a brand new lap top computer with speech synthesiser, paid for by our Primary Care Trust. I am sure agreement to purchase this was due in no small measure to sterling work by Kirsty, an excellent speech therapist, who showed such determination and patience whilst helping Peter. It was a big advantage to have a portable machine because he could use it away from his own home and take part in general conversations. Of course, access was still limited to use of the eyebrow switching system being attached to his spectacles. He had tried many other ideas for securing the eyebrow switch including a head band, a cap and a visor but they all moved slightly when in use so were not suitable for him. His glasses were the most comfortable and reliable method of housing for the switch. The lap top was purchased through Cambridge Adaptive Communications who had been involved with looking after his equipment for many years although they were now part of the Possum Charity. This company had also supplied Professor Stephen Hawking, the eminent scientist who wrote 'A brief history of Time', with his portable computer and speech synthesiser which was fixed to his wheelchair. I think somehow Peter would like to have joined him floating in space but this venture came too late for our son to even contemplate, I'm afraid.

As the twentieth anniversary of his accident approached in September, 2002, he decided it was appropriate to write a few letters of thanks to some of the professional people who had helped him in the early days. He wrote to Dr. Frankel at Stoke Mandeville and Mr. Peter Teddy to say how much he had appreciated their efforts on his behalf. He said their skill had given him nearly twenty years of happy ventilator free life. I know he also wrote to Sir Jimmy Savile thanking him for his kindness and generosity, in arranging the funding side of things. Maybe he shouldn't have boasted about how well he was doing or did he actually have an inkling the implants would not last for very much longer?

Whether this was so or not, by the winter of 2002/3, Peter's breathing was starting to cause us all great anxiety. His diaphragmatic pacemakers did not seem nearly so efficient and as a result, his oxygen levels were suffering. Chest infections were becoming increasingly frequent for him and he no sooner finished one course of antibiotics before it became necessary to start another one. Did this mean that his lungs were becoming fatigued with the constant stimulation required by the pacemaker system? Peter was sure this was not so and that the problem originated from the implants in his lungs. He felt they required replacing but the medics were not so certain and he needed to convince them before they were prepared to take any action in this regard.

However, events overtook any discussions about this because Peter developed an extremely severe bout of pneumonia. We had an urgent call from the carer on duty during the afternoon of the 2nd April, 2003 to say she was very anxious about his health. His condition had suddenly deteriorated during the day to such an extent she felt he should be admitted to hospital as a matter of extreme urgency. Lane Fox Unit did not have a bed available and so he was taken to Whipps Cross Accident and Emergency Department from where he was immediately transferred to their Intensive Therapy Unit. Here the medical staff were so alarmed at his diaphragmatic weakness they gave him no alternative. He would have to be connected to a ventilator or they would not be responsible for the outcome. Peter was very distressed but in no position to argue. There were no facilities here for his carers to become part of the team looking after him and he felt isolated. Fortunately it was only a couple of days before he could be transferred to St. Thomas' Hospital but he had to make the journey by ambulance without the support of one of his carers who would have been able to speak for him. When he did finally arrive, he was too ill to go straight to the Lane Fox Unit. He needed to spend a couple of days in St. Thomas' intensive care department before he could take up the bed allocated to him on Lane Fox. Still at least he felt a little more comfortable here because there was provision for his own girls to be part of his care team.

As we had already suspected, it appeared that food and drink had got into his lungs whilst his breathing was so poor which was of course extremely dangerous. Ideally, he should be tube fed but Peter was determined he was not going to stop eating or drinking the same way as the rest of us did. Culinary delights and liquid refreshments were two of his greatest pleasures and he did not intend to give them up. The medics supervising his care had to explain the risks he was taking but they respected his wishes and he battled on. He was given intensive physiotherapy, using an oscillator to keep his lungs clear of debris but for the time being the ventilator had to stay. He felt that the vibrating of his chest caused by the oscillator was moving his implants and impairing their function but this was never proved.

This time he had to spend three months on the Lane Fox Unit before he was well enough to be considered for discharge. He was, however, still completely dependent on a ventilator for breathing and before he could actually go home, all his carers had to receive extensive training on what had now become a vital piece of apparatus for his survival. I know Peter himself wasn't at all happy about having to use this machine. As far as he was concerned, it was a terrible retrograde step. His life was restricted enough already but if he was forced to use a ventilator, would he ever be able to do anything or go anywhere? On a positive note, investigations were to be carried out to see whether he could have new implants fitted and so avoid the necessity of the ventilator some time in the not too distant future. Hira, the senior technician on the unit was brilliant and he liaised with the

Dobelle Institute in the United States of America to formulate a plan.

St. Thomas' Hospital was now linked with Guys and they were expecting a French surgeon to be seconded to them in the next few months. This man had experience of diaphragmatic pacemakers and when he arrived at Guys, Peter's case would be discussed with him. Meanwhile the machine would have to continue supplying his lungs with air if he wanted to stay alive. He also had to have a new bed at home with more accessories and a special trolley to accommodate all the extra equipment that had become necessary for his continued existence. Our NHS Trust pulled out all the stops for him and his new bed was delivered the very same day he was allowed to come home. The new trolley followed shortly after.

Although he had so looked forward to being back in his own home, I know it wasn't quite the joyous occasion he had envisaged. At first, he couldn't even take pleasure in the luxury of being showered and having his hair washed in his own bathroom, because the ventilator had to remain plugged in at all times. He would have to wait for longer tubing to arrive so the consequences of mixing live electricity with water could be avoided.

In typical Peter fashion, he didn't stay dejected for long and was soon working with his carers thinking up ways he could get out and about again. The wheelchair service promptly arranged the necessary strengthening of his chair so it was safe to carry the ventilator on a tray at the back of his wheelchair without the whole thing becoming top-heavy. The ventilator wasn't a problem in the car because he had a very large portable battery he could use. He just needed an electricity supply when he arrived at his destination. I remember one of his first trips, apart from visits to other people's houses, was to a scout fun day. Most of our family went to this annual fund raising event, where there was music, activities for the children, a beer tent for the adults and a huge barbecue for one and all. The lead for Peter's ventilator had to trail across the grass from the electricity supply rigged up for the P.A. system but at least he was able to enjoy the day in his usual style.

By being a bit resourceful, it was possible to overcome most of the extra problems the ventilator had caused. He would have liked to go on holiday but decided it was probably best to wait until after his meeting with the French surgeon before making any plans. However, when this meeting was delayed, Peter became impatient and wanted to get away for a break. I must admit to feeling a bit scared at the prospects of having something go wrong in a foreign country and so in the end we compromised; we returned to Devon, where he had enjoyed happy holidays in the past. This was to be his last holiday I'm afraid but at least he enjoyed it and had the company of Julie, Fergie and their three boys.

Finally, he was given an appointment to meet Mr. Lang-Lazdunski (the French surgeon) in August 2004 and replacement of his implants was eventually carried out the following month at Guys hospital. The operation was successful but of course there now followed a long period retraining his body to accept pacer stimulation again. At first he could only use the pacers for a few minutes twice a day but gradually this was increased until he could manage all day just returning to the ventilator at night. I think he was reasonably happy with this and didn't want to push for full twenty four hour pacing in case something went wrong again.

In hindsight, I don't think his oxygen levels were ever as good as they were originally when he was pacing. Now he was reliant on the extra boost the ventilator gave him overnight to carry him through the following day. Still he never complained and just enjoyed his slightly increased freedom from the dreaded machine for what was to be the last few months of his life.

His beloved red Ford Galaxy.

Showing back open with ramp for Peter

With Debbie at Scout Barbeque in spite of ventilator

Still managing to enjoy a glass of vino.

On holiday in Devon for the last time

The view from our bungalow at Blagdon farm, Devon.

213

Back to St. Thomas'

There was nothing really to indicate that Peter's life was drawing to a close at this time. On the 28th April, Karen called me in the morning to say she didn't think Peter was all that great. His oxygen levels were poor and she felt he needed checking over. Unfortunately, Lane Fox Ward was full and therefore, we called an ambulance and he was taken to Whipps Cross Hospital Accident & Emergency Department for treatment. His breathing deteriorated even further over the next few hours and for the first time ever, the next day he was actually admitted to an ordinary ward at Whipps Cross as there was no bed for him on the intensive care unit. Peter didn't really feel safe here as the nursing staff were unfamiliar with his ventilator and had no experience of treating someone with his special needs. Although his own carers were with him during the **day,** there wasn't anywhere for them to sleep at night so he was at the mercy of the nursing staff on the ward itself. They couldn't understand his method of communication or exactly how his own apparatus worked. He sent me a message outlining his fears and we went to see the consultant on intensive care that evening. He promised to keep an eye on Peter throughout the night and we all felt slightly happier. It was the May bank holiday weekend, staff levels were low and the ward was heavily reliant on agency personnel.

There was still no room for Peter on the Lane Fox Unit so we had to keep our fingers crossed and just hope for the best.

He didn't get any worse although there didn't seem to be much improvement in his condition either. His sense of humour hadn't deserted him though. It was a mixed unit and there was one poor demented soul who wandered up and down the ward in her flimsy nightdress, whenever the opportunity presented itself. Peter said to me, every time she passes by, I whistle in my head the tune to 'The Great Escape'.

Exactly one week later, in the afternoon of the 5th May, he was discharged home. Karen was working again that day and although she was a really experienced carer, she didn't feel at all happy about his condition and neither did the rest of us. He had been prescribed an oxygen cylinder for use in case of an emergency at home but owing to a mix-up between hospital and chemist, this never actually arrived.

Dave and I were back at Peter's home during the early evening and before midnight we had to call an ambulance. Once more he was taken to the Accident and Emergency department of Whipps Cross Hospital. However, he wasn't actually seen by a doctor until around 5 a.m. the next morning. We were told that because he had only been discharged from a ward a few hours earlier, the correct procedure was for the ward doctor to come and assess him. Karen had Peter's own equipment with her and was monitoring his oxygen levels herself. Throughout the rest of that night his condition deteriorated further and even the doctor in charge on the Accident and Emergency ward was getting very frustrated that nobody had appeared from the ward in spite of his many requests for their Houseman to come and see Peter. Eventually, the emergency doctor chose to ignore the rules and examined Peter himself arranging for his admission. This time he was allocated a bed on the day unit of A & E. His colour and breathing were not good and we felt very worried. A broncoscopy was carried out around midday and then to the relief of us all, there was a telephone call from St. Thomas' to say they now had room for Peter on the Lane Fox Unit. By lunch time on the 7th he was being greeted as an old friend on the newly refurbished Lane Fox Unit. He seemed to improve straight away under their expert care. He didn't manage to get home for his birthday on the 9th but the staff helped us all celebrate as did a lot of family members. A big cake was provided for him and we all sang happy birthday. He definitely seemed better and wanted to know what was on at the 'Medi-cinema' at St. Thomas'. (This was the in-house cinema for patients and their families actually based within the hospital itself) Yes, he thought he would go there on Wednesday, the 11th when Karin, his South African carer was working. She would like the film they were showing that day and so would he. Sadly this was not to be. At 7 a.m. on the 10th May, we had a call from the hospital. Karen was in tears and said the doctor wanted to talk to us. He thought Peter had suffered a sort of epileptic seizure/stroke and wasn't really conscious at present. We hurried back to London. Scans showed massive damage to his brain and we began to think that this time, maybe he wasn't going to make it. He died at 6.21 pm on Thursday 12th May, just two weeks after his initial admission to Whipps Cross.

He didn't really regain consciousness during these final days but sometimes his eyes were open as though he was looking at us all and he appeared peaceful. The doctors and nurses on the ward were wonderful, looking after us with practical help and support.   All his carers, family and friends were able to come and say goodbye to a most remarkable, spirited and inspirational young man.   I looked round at his birthday cards, still on the wall around his bed; the usual assortment that Peter loved – drawings from his various young friends; sexy or double meaning jokes from his contemporaries and even ones poking fun at his disabilities. He never wanted pity – just to be allowed to get on with his life as normally as possible.

This was the way he would have chosen to go I feel sure; surrounded by his family and friends, pain free and not having to be compelled to spend his remaining years in an institution, totally dependent on society and the state for his very existence. Maybe it was the right time for the end of his life to come, whilst he could still issue orders and basically be in control of his own destiny. Dave and I were getting older and I am not sure how long we could have continued to oversee his care package, which gave him the opportunity to live as normally as possible in the community.

One does not expect their children to leave this earth before their own time comes, but Peter, you must know you were very special to us; you will never be forgotten. Although your life was only short, it was such a good and rewarding one. You will always be remembered by so many people, including those whose own lives were influenced by the way you lived yours.

**Edward outside Lane Fox –
Note: view including Houses of Parliament and Big Ben**

The Final Chapter

Peter's brother David had written lovely individual and personal letters to all the girls who worked for him, managing to highlight their own special attributes. They were going to find it very hard to come to terms with their lives without their boss and on a practical note, they now didn't have jobs. They had no paper qualifications and yet were probably some of the best trained care assistants in the country.

We stayed very close and helped each other. We all met at Peter's flat the next day to attend to urgent business. The girls sorted and packed the medical equipment and drugs ready for return. Karen offered to take Peter's wheelchair back to the NHS, and Linda had found a new home for Florence, the cat. We would have to clear the flat out and return the keys, but not until after his funeral. The next job was to look at Peter's computer. We were all quite surprised to find he had left a message on it for everyone and I make no excuse for including this now. (After all, it is Peter's book and he must have the last say).

'I have very much enjoyed my life, both in and out of the wheelchair, especially with my family and as a teenager and even at school – (not during lessons mind).

Although being handicapped, I have not been prevented from doing or wanting anything.

I still managed to do my favourite hobby of travelling and have often been to America and various places around Europe.

When I was a bit younger, I also went to hundreds of concerts.

All this and more is due to my family.'

Just to add that I am sure he would have approved of his funeral. He had left very specific instructions about the form it was to take and even a Compact Disc pre-recorded with the music he wanted played at the Service:

No woman, no cry	(Bob Marley)
You do something to me	(Paul Weller)
The long and winding road	(The Beatles)
Against all Odds	(Phil Collins)
Fly me to the moon	(Frank Sinatra)

It was to be a celebration of his life, not a miserable occasion.

The Church was filled not only with family and friends but also many of the professional people Peter had met along the way since his accident. Doctors, Nurses, Therapists, Social Service and Health Authority staff all agreed; Peter was such an inspirational character and had created such a lasting impression on them, he would influence the way they dealt with other disabled people for the rest of their working life.

Acknowledgements

Peter's happy life following his horrendous accident would not have been possible if it had not been for the tremendous support he and indeed we, received from so many other people and the various charitable and statutory bodies involved in his care.

First and foremost our thanks must go to our family. Not only did they always try and include Peter in their plans, but they also supported my husband and I, stepping in whenever they could, helping out and encouraging us to have a break from caring.

Secondly, great thanks are due to all the girls who were such brilliant carers for Peter over the years he lived in his own home. Working for Peter was far more than a job for each of them and they did much to enhance the quality of his life whilst they were with him.

We really appreciate the dedication of the hospital staff at the various places where Peter was cared for, particularly

Stoke Mandeville and the Lane Fox Unit of St. Thomas' Hospital. It was not just the expertise of the staff and technical support services, which is beyond question but also their wonderful understanding of how to maintain Peter's dignity and independence of spirit. I must also include here the Young Disabled Unit at Chingford Hospital and their extremely understanding and tolerant unit manager, Joan Corry. What a tragedy that this establishment had to be closed due to cuts in the NHS budget.

Our local health authority – now Waltham Forest Primary Care Trust also deserve special thanks. Without their funding, we could never have managed. They, too, were pioneers. When Peter first came into the Community, 'Independent Living' didn't really mean much. At that time, I only knew of one other health authority in the country funding disabled people to enable them to live in their own homes but even they didn't cater for persons with such multiple disabilities as those suffered by Peter. Waltham Forest P.C.T. created a package to be proud of including many ancillary services and a model for other Health Authorities/Primary Care Trusts/Social Service Departments to follow.

Over the years, the Spinal Injuries Association provided very useful practical support and information whenever we needed guidance as to the best way to proceed. I would thoroughly recommend this association to anyone who has suffered a spinal injury.

Another organisation worthy of praise in its support of all disabled people and their helpers is the Carer's Association. When things are difficult and you are feeling low, it is comforting to be able to talk to other people facing problems somewhat similar to your own. We found their advice and support invaluable. They have branches all over the country.

Finally, there were many individuals who enriched Peter's life over the ensuing years following his accident. I have tried to acknowledge their valuable help in the body of this book but would also like to document our grateful thanks to all the professional people who helped Peter and us, his family. Without you, his happy life would not have been possible.

Peter - doing the things he loved best

Working at his computer

Being on holiday with family and friends

With animals   or   with kids

or at a family gathering

ISBN 1425147305
9 781425 147303